LOVE AND AWAKENING

LOVE AND AWAKENING

Discovering the Sacred Path of

Intimate Relationship

John Welwood

HarperPerennial
A Division of HarperCollinsPublishers

A hardcover edition of this book was published in 1996 by HarperCollins Publishers.

Grateful acknowledgment is made to the following for permission to reprint portions of copyrighted material:

EAST WEST PUBLICATIONS: From "The Circle," by Rabindranath Tagore, translated by P. Bowes. Reprinted with permission of East West Publications from *Some Songs and Poems from Rabindranath Tagore*, translated by P. Bowes. Copyright © 1984 by East West Publications.

ROBERT BLY: From "Last Night," by Antonio Machado, translated by Robert Bly. From *Times Alone: Selected Poems of Antonio Machado*, translated by Robert Bly. Wesleyan University Press. Copyright © 1983 by Robert Bly, reprinted with his permission.

SIMON & SCHUSTER: From "Vacillation," by W. B. Yeats. Excerpted with the permission of Simon & Schuster, Inc., from *The Poems of W. B. Yeats: A New Edition*, edited by Richard J. Finneran. Copyright © 1993 by Macmillan Publishing Company, renewed by Bertha Georgie Yeats.

HarperCollins books may be purchased for educational, business, or sales promotional use. For information, please e-mail the Special Markets Department at SPsales@harpercollins.com.

First HarperPerennial edition published 1997.

Designed by Laura Lindgren

The Library of Congress has catalogued the hardcover edition as follows:

Welwood, John, 1943–
    Love and awakening : discovering the sacred path of intimate relationship / John Welwood. — 1st. ed.
      p.   cm.
    Includes bibliographical references (p. 254).
    ISBN 0-06-017269-X
    1. Man-woman relationships. 2. Love. 3. Intimacy (Psychology). 4. Self-actualization (Psychology). I. Title.
HQ801.W637   1996
158'.2—dc20   95-46903

ISBN 0-06-092797-6 (pbk.)

HB 12.13.2022

For Jennifer

CONTENTS

Most people in our society share a peculiar belief: We imagine that we should be able to establish a rich and satisfying relationship with someone we love, even if we have never learned to relate to ourselves in a rich, satisfying way. We believe that a successful relationship mostly depends on finding the right person and feeling or doing the right things. We often don't see that how we relate to another inevitably follows from how we relate to ourselves, that our outer relationships are but an extension of our inner life, that we can only be as open and present with another as we are with ourselves.

Thirty years ago a powerful consciousness-raising movement came into prominence in America as women began challenging all the old roles and stereotypes that blocked their development. More recently, an emerging men's movement has brought into question the old orthodoxies about what it means to be a man. Now that men and women have separately explored these issues, we have finally reached the point where we can ask, from a fresh perspective: *What is a couple,* aside from the old myths and stereotypes? What is the purpose of two people committing themselves to a life together, beyond just raising children or making a cozy home? What are two people who love each other really meant to do together? Now that the old social mandates have largely disappeared and the romantic dream of living happily ever after hasn't lived up to its promise, couple consciousness at the end of the millennium is finally ready to find a new maturity and a deeper sense of purpose. *The time is ripe for couples' consciousness-raising.*

The increasingly precarious state of our planet and its inhabitants is calling on us to wake up, reevaluate how we are living, and align ourselves with a larger, sacred vision of human life. While this kind of self-inquiry used to be the vocation of spiritual adepts, who often left the world behind in pursuit of truth, we can no longer afford the luxury of a spirituality that is divorced from "real life." In these times when our world and our very humanity are increasingly at risk, we need a new kind of grounded spirituality that arises out of, and addresses itself to, the challenges of ordinary living. We need a grounded spirituality that can transform the quality of life on this planet through being thoroughly committed to the here-and-now. Fortunately, we have a powerful vehicle close at hand for developing this kind of wisdom—our intimate relations with those we love.

Yet our relationships themselves are also in desperate need of reassessment. With the old reasons for marriage no longer so compelling, with so many families falling apart and couples of all persuasions finding it difficult to build a life together, we need to re-vision the purpose of intimate relationship from the ground up. We need a new understanding of what relationship can truly offer, as well as what makes it so difficult. And we need to see how this difficulty can serve as the grist for real self-knowledge—which is the key to connecting with ourselves and others in a more satisfying way. The art of love requires something that has never been fully explored or articulated before: *a sacred psychology of the couple.*

According to an ancient truth, known as the "law of three," every relationship consists of a trinity: two poles and an overarching purpose or reconciling principle that binds them together. Always before, *external social mandates* provided this stabilizing third element: Marriage had a clearly defined *function* in serving family and society. Yet now that marriage is based instead on two people looking to one another for pleasure, comfort, and need-gratification—*subjective feeling states* that inevitably come and go—it lacks a critical binding element, especially in times when pain and discomfort inevitably arise.

As soon as we look beyond both duty and pleasure for a deeper meaning and purpose in relationships today, we start to move in the direction of the sacred, which we could define as *coming into deeper connection with our true, essential nature,* behind all our masks and facades. This book will show how, when two partners join together in awakening and honoring the presence of the sacred in their life together, this can serve as a binding force to provide direction, meaning, and purpose that will continue to unfold over a lifetime.

Although "awakening to the sacred" might sound esoteric, it is, in fact, quite ordinary—for it only involves learning to respond more deeply to what we already experience, and to appreciate what we *already essentially are.* If the bad news is that we can know another, and be known, only as deeply as we know ourselves—and coming to know ourselves can be a long and arduous journey—the good news is that love helps and inspires us to develop this deeper self-knowledge. How we relate to someone we love, as we shall see, provides an extremely clear and accurate mirror of how we relate to ourselves. For this reason, relationships can help us face ourselves and understand ourselves more rapidly and profoundly than any other aspect of worldly life. Seen in this light, love becomes a path of *awakening*—rousing us from the sleep of old, unconscious patterns into the freshness and immediacy of living more fully in the present, in accord with who we really are. *This* is the source of a deeper kind of happiness, which goes far beyond pleasure and comfort, and the only real basis for healthy and satisfying relationships.

Love and Awakening, like its predecessor, *Journey of the Heart*, arose out of my own pressing need to find a new way to be in a relationship. When I first began this inquiry, two decades ago, I sought in vain in the areas of psychology, philosophy, and spirituality, East and West, for a teaching that would illuminate the subtle, multidimensional play that happens between two individuals who, each in themselves, are a mysterious blend of body, mind, soul, and spirit. Eventually I realized I would have to find my own path, and develop my own understanding of this whole area, which had never been fully explored or articulated before.

This book is a further step in that direction, offering an approach to relationships that is significantly different from the standard approaches currently available. Most conventional relationship strategies focus on problem-solving. They prescribe techniques for how to communicate, how to have better sex, how to stop being codependent, how to fight or not fight, how to handle gender differences, or how to survive the divorce. Obviously, such techniques can have value. But the "fix-it" approach also fosters a mindset in which we imagine that the answers to our problems are to be found outside us—in some formula or procedure—rather than within us—in our own deepest resources. And this prevents us from recognizing love's larger, sacred potential—the opportunities its challenges provide for deepening our connection with ourselves, our partner, and life as a whole.

At the other end of the spectrum we find the "inspirational" or New Age approach, offering lofty visions—of letting go of fear, surrendering to love, opening the heart, seeing God in one's partner—without, however, addressing the real psychological difficulties that relationships bring to the fore. This approach places the sacred in some higher realm that can only be reached by *transcending* or *bypassing* complex emotional, real-life issues—what I call "spiritual bypassing." Thus it fails to provide a *path* or method for working with love's challenges and discovering their transformative potential. If the conventional approach is all earth, no heaven, the new age approach is, in effect, all heaven, no earth.

Love and Awakening, by contrast, presents an integrated *psychospiritual approach,* providing both a larger vision and a practical method, or path, for realizing that vision. The first half of the book shows how *every psychological obstacle in a relationship provides a special kind of spiritual opportunity,* which few other aspects of our lives offer in such a powerful way. As love opens us up, it also brings us up against fears and resistances that cause us to contract and shut down. If we are to keep expanding under love's influence, we need to learn how to negotiate this tension between expansion and contraction, which love intensifies. The early chapters (2–8) focus on this central theme from a number of different angles, while the later chapters (9–14) focus on the expansive possibilities of relationship more directly.

This book also introduces a unique format: I have included experiential dialogues from relationship workshops, in order to bring home, in a highly practical and personal way, main ideas in the chapter preceding them. These dialogues also illustrate a simple, direct method for going to the heart of whatever one is struggling with in a relationship, and in so doing, becoming more fully present with oneself and one's partner. This method belongs to an overall approach that I call "Presence-Centered Psychotherapy™," which will form the subject of a future book.

A few specific points bear mentioning here:

While my previous book *Journey of the Heart* provided an overview of conscious relationship, covering a wide range of issues such as passion, surrender, commitment, marriage, and sex, *Love and Awakening* focuses more specifically on relationship as a vehicle for recovering lost dimensions of our being. Yet though this work covers new and different ground, the two books necessarily share certain themes. They are designed to work in tandem, so that readers of either one will find that the other takes them further. I have provided cross-references between the two books, as well as other more detailed discussions that digress from the main flow of the text, in the notes at the conclusion of this volume.

The examples I have drawn on from my psychotherapy practice are not meant as clinical studies, but rather as highly condensed, distilled examples designed to illustrate certain points. Likewise, my presentation of child development is not meant to be comprehensive, but only to bring out certain key issues relevant to the themes addressed in these pages.

While this work primarily focuses on heterosexual couples, it is not meant to exclude same-sex partners. I concentrate on heterosexual relationship because this is where my personal interest and experience lie, but I believe that most of what I discuss here will also prove relevant for same-sex couples.

The ideas and understandings set forth in this book are meant to apply only to relationships where two partners share a deep connection, a willingness to work with its challenges, and a commitment to their own unfolding. This material should not be used as a rationale for staying in a relationship where these elements are missing, or where good faith and goodwill are absent.

My greatest wish is that *Love and Awakening* will help you forge your own larger vision of intimate relationship and discover its sacred potential. There is no time to lose. Only between one person and another can the renewal of our world begin.

Chapter One

WE NEED A NEW VISION

Being is presence. To recognize this is wisdom and freedom.

H. L. POONJA

In every relationship the question eventually arises: "What am I doing here? Is it really worth the struggle?" Such concerns might surface in the first week of being together, or after years or decades. But sooner or later, when a relationship starts to feel more like work than fun, we begin to wonder if we are on the right track. Why keep going when the initial excitement fades or when we keep hurting each other? Or when intimacy with another exposes parts of ourselves we would rather not look at? Or when we start to doubt whether we have what it takes to live with another person, or to love anybody at all on a daily basis?

Finding our way through the complexities of intimacy today is like being lost in the wilderness without a map or compass. Much of the time we are busy tending wounds we have suffered while stumbling blindly through the underbrush. Yet though bandaging our wounds may bring temporary relief, it does not address the basic problem: We can't find our way *because we don't know where we are going*. We have a hard time working with love's challenges because we lack a clear sense of what relationships are about anymore. What we need, more than any quick fix or temporary solution, is a new guiding vision of the meaning and purpose of long-term relationship.

All significant achievements come about through vision and intention. No one—whether an artist, a mountain climber, a yogi, or an entrepreneur—can persist in a long, arduous undertaking without a vision of what he or she wants to realize. Having a vision, along with a clear intention to manifest that vision, helps us persevere in the face of obstacles that inevitably arise. Yet often we enter relationships without knowing what it is we really want. Without a sense of what we're after, we will not understand why it is meaningful to work with the difficulties encountered on the path of love, and are thus likely to lose heart along the way.

Natural Presence

One way to start forging a new vision of relationship is simply by asking ourselves what we most cherish in our connection with another person. When working with couples in groups, I often start by inviting them to tell me what they most enjoy about falling in love. What makes it feel so wonderful, so powerful and compelling? What does it give them that they value beyond all else? Some of the answers I often hear are:

- A feeling of being part of something larger
- A deeper sense of being myself, being who I really am
- A new kind of strength and peace
- A sense of life's magic

- No longer fearing the unknown
- A flowing movement and connectedness
- A fresh acceptance of myself and everything
- Being more alive in my body and senses
- Seeing the world with new eyes
- Feeling blessed
- Coming home

And when I ask people what qualities being in love puts them in touch with, they mention warmth, innocence, gratitude, passion, kindness, expansiveness, realness, trust, beauty, wonder, openness, delight, affirmation, richness, integrity, power.

All of these statements point in the same direction. When we are in love, *we become more fully present*, more connected with ourselves and the world around us. In moments of heightened presence we no longer need to prove ourselves. Something in us relaxes. Our usual cares and distractions fade into the background, and we feel more awake, more alive. We experience what it is like *just to be present, just to be ourselves*. Falling in love is powerful and enlivening because it opens us to our larger being.

As a noun, the word *being* can sound static or abstract. But if we consider it as a verb form—*be-ing*—it denotes the living process that we are, an immediate coming-into-presence and engaging with what is. A simple way to glimpse the nature of your being is to ask yourself as you read this, "Who is taking in these words? Who is experiencing all of this right now?" Without trying to *think* of an answer, if you look directly into the experiencer, the experiencing consciousness itself, what you find is a silent presence that has no shape, location, or form. This nameless, formless presence—in, around, behind, and between all our particular thoughts and experiences—is what the great spiritual traditions regard as our true nature, or home-ground, also known as the essential self or holy spirit.

3

Be-ing means resting in the flow of this presence, which is awake, open, and responsive to reality—described by the Christian mystic Meister Eckhart as "now-flowing." This dynamic, fluid openness provides a *direct* channel to the heart of life, in contrast to the *indirect* ways we usually relate to things—through mental activity and emotional reactivity. That is why falling in love feels like coming home—it helps us enter the flow of being, which is the only true and reliable resting place we can find on this earth.

The Tibetan teacher Chögyam Trungpa had a revealing term for this quality of open presence that is our essential nature. He called it *basic goodness*. Though we may spend much of our time and energy trying to prove our worth, the truth is that our nature already contains its own intrinsic, unconditional value.

This is not to say that people are only good—which would be naive, considering all the evil that humans perpetrate in this world. Our unconditional value lies much deeper than our conditioned personality and behavior, which are always a mix of positive and negative tendencies. It lies in the essential openness at the core of our nature, which allows us to know and experience value in ourselves and the world around us. Our capacity for open presence is the source not only of value but of all the other positive human qualities as well—joy, kindness, courage, aliveness, authenticity—that people experience so vividly when they are in love. These qualities are the flavors of basic goodness, the ways it manifests in our life.

The openness at the core of our being allows us to appreciate existence as basically good, even in the most trying circumstances. It allows us to see the ordinary magic of things as they are. From this perspective, all the evils in the world are the result of not recognizing, or having faith in, this essential ground of our existence.

We can directly perceive this wholesome quality of our existence in moments when we feel the sheer immediacy and delight of being alive. One day William Butler Yeats, sitting in a crowded London tea shop, had a vivid experience of this, describing it as a moment of great simplicity, grace, and benediction streaming through his whole body:

> *While on the shop and street I gazed*
> *My body of a sudden blazed;*
> *And twenty minutes more or less*
> *It seemed, so great a happiness,*
> *That I was blessèd and could bless.*

Love inspires us to relax into the blessèd flow of our being. That is why we value it so. What we most cherish with our loved ones are experiences of *just being* together. All our deepest, intimate moments are those in which we're simply present—being ourselves, and sharing the richness of that with someone we love. Not so much being *together* as *being* together.

Our culture teaches us a great deal about having and doing, but very little about this kind of *being*. When we focus on a relationship as something to *have*, it becomes something to hold on to, a box with walls, rather than something vast and boundless. When we focus on relationship as something to *do*, it becomes busy and effortful—which destroys its freshness and spontaneity. Beyond all the particular things two people *have* or *do* together, their deepest connection is the quality of being they experience in each other's presence.

Only in this stillpoint of presence can we really appreciate our life. Indeed, the things we most enjoy—lovemaking, natural beauty, creative challenges, sports or strenuous exercise—are those that bring us alive and fully here. And when we are fully here, we taste our true nature—that quality of open presence which is homeground, the source of all joy and fulfillment.

Presence is like the air we breathe—essential for our life, yet so transparent and intangible that we rarely give it particular attention or importance. As a writer, I can easily become fixated on the results and rewards of my work—the finished product—and fail to see that its value for me also lies in bringing me into a more focused type of presence, where I tap into a deeper knowing within. If, as I write, I do not pay attention to this flow of being, I lose my enjoyment of the process, along with most of my effectiveness. When athletes become caught up in hopes and fears about success or failure, they lose their poise, and often the game as well. Similarly, when lovers lose the grace of heightened presence and become caught up in the distractions of daily life, the joy of relating to each other soon starts to fade.

As a psychotherapist, I find that married couples have often completely lost this key to the treasure of the heart—simple presence. They may love one another deeply, yet when they sit side by side on the couch in my office, *they are not really there with each other*. Separated by outer obstacles—the busyness of their lives, the pressures they are under—and by inner obstacles—old beliefs about themselves and each other, emotional reactions, fears, and patterns of denial and avoidance—they have lost contact with the vibrant aliveness that first attracted them to each other.

Refining the Gold

Falling in love provides a glimpse of the real gold that lies at the heart of our humanness. In love's early stages, powerful qualities of our being—openness, peace, expansiveness, delight—simply emerge, unbidden, out of the heightened sense of presence we experience with our partner. And this inspires us to commit ourselves more fully to this growing connection, which seems to bring so many blessings.

Yet as the relationship proceeds, the gold often becomes harder and harder to find. Old personality patterns, which are like iron ore mixed in with the gold, begin to obscure it. If we want to regain access to the pure gold, we will have to go through a refining process—which involves encountering and working with our obscurations. In fact, the obstacles to loving presence contained within us *need* to come up and be worked with if we are to free ourselves from them.

If falling in love provides a glimpse of our true nature, entering into a long-term relationship brings us up against all the obstacles to residing there—whatever prevents us from being present, being real, being ourselves. I don't know any couples who have not suffered this fall from grace at some point, losing touch with the original bright presence that first drew them together. Yet this is not a problem when we understand it as an integral part of a couple's journey toward greater wholeness and a richer, more seasoned kind of love.

The Sufi tradition contains an important distinction between *states*—qualities of being, like peace, joy, trust, inner strength, or confidence, which emerge spontaneously for a short time, as when we fall in love—and *stations*—these same qualities when they have become permanently integrated into our lives. Once a state has passed, we cannot readily call it back. But a quality that has become a station is one we have access to whenever it is needed. If love and presence are to become stations in our lives and in our relationships, rather than just passing states, we need to understand what we do to obstruct them, and how we can remove these obstructions. This is the path of conscious relationship.

When two partners with a deep bond choose to work with the obstacles arising between them, this deepens their connection with themselves and each other, and can provide a lifelong, mutual sense of path and direction. On the other hand, if they refuse to work with the difficulties in their relationship, they lose a precious opportunity to let the fire of their love refine their natures and forge their inner gold. One of the chief sins against loving, according to the Sufi master Hazrat Inayat Khan, is "shrinking from all the sorrows, pains, troubles, and difficulties that come in the path of love."

Of course, facing the challenges on this path takes great courage and daring. This is where a guiding vision becomes essential: It helps two partners take heart and gather their energies when they feel lost or bogged down. What can sustain a couple through the most difficult times is knowing that they are together for a larger purpose— helping each other refine the gold of their essential natures by working through obstacles in the way of their deepest unfolding. Such a vision can help them convert ordinary tribulations into what the Russian teacher Gurd-jieff called "conscious suffering"—willingly making use of the pain of encountering inner obstacles, as motivation to work on overcoming them.

Now that many of the traditional bonds holding couples together have broken down, relationships can thrive in these difficult times only if they *reflect and promote our true nature*. This is the kind of connection our heart truly desires. Do you really want a partnership that reflects and promotes only your personality, your concepts and beliefs about yourself—who you *think* you are? That is an unconscious relationship, based on ignoring and denying aspects of yourself that don't fit some image in your mind. A conscious relationship is one that calls forth who you *really* are. It is dedicated to truth, rather than to chasing after illusory images. Regarding relationship as a vehicle or path that can help two people access the powerful qualities of their true nature provides the new vision our age so urgently needs.

Chapter Two

LOVE AND AWAKENING

While most of us enter relationships somewhat unconsciously—without understanding what we're getting ourselves in for—the challenges of forging an authentic connection with another person inevitably spur us to become more conscious, to examine ourselves more deeply, and to develop greater intention, courage, and awareness in the way we live. Hermann Hesse wrote a beautiful story about this—in which a man's attraction to his beloved completely transforms him, by compelling him to set out in search of himself and his true aim in life.

The story begins with Anselm as a young boy who is captivated by the irises in his mother's garden, and ends with his life-altering attraction as an adult to a woman named Iris. Both attractions—to the flower and to the woman—serve as pathways into his own soul. But like most of us, Anselm does not recognize that his romantic attraction contains this deeper impulse—to connect with what is most real inside himself.

As a child, Anselm experiences the magic of being alive most vividly when he is in the garden, communing with butterflies and pebbles, making friends with beetles and lizards, and taking special delight in the iris:

> When he stared into her chalice and allowed his thoughts to follow that bright path toward the twilight interior of the flower, his soul looked through the gate of a heavenly palace, and with him glided gently the whole world drawn by magic into the lovely abyss, inward and downward, where every wish found fulfillment and every intimation came true.

Through contemplating the secret recesses of the iris, Anselm is unwittingly connecting with the depth of his soul, an inner movement described by Mirra Alfassa, a close associate of the Indian sage Aurobindo:

> To find the soul one must step back from the surface, [go] deep within, and enter, enter ... and then there is something warm, tranquil, rich, very still, and very full, like a sweetness—this is the soul.

This kind of movement from surface to depth reveals the source of all fulfillment in life—the essential aliveness and presence at the core of our nature, whose great beauty and abundance are described in certain spiritual traditions as a "wish-fulfilling gem" or "jewel beyond all price."

Like Anselm, we all enter this world possessing an intrinsic radiance that shines forth from our inner core. We are born into a vast palace of powers and possibilities; our being contains boundless potential. From deep within us we can bring forth a wide range of resources, such as strength, wisdom, compassion, tenderness, joy, humor, and generosity. This is our divine birthright. As children, most of us have some intimation—if only for a few brief, shining moments—that we arrive here "trailing clouds of glory as we come."

Loss of Being: Closing down the Palace

Yet we are also born into a complex emotional world—our family and society—in a state of total vulnerability. We need adults not only to meet our basic physical and emotional needs, but also to serve as a mirror—to see us clearly, to respond appropriately to our feelings, to reflect back to us, thus helping us see our core goodness and potential. That kind of mirroring would help us begin to know and appreciate ourselves, and encourage our unfolding. Though as children we may sense our true nature, we lack the capacity to fully recognize or comprehend its significance, to appreciate that we *are* that very fullness, glory, and beauty. We have not yet developed the self-reflective awareness that would allow us to know ourselves in this way.

Unfortunately, most parents cannot help their children recognize or honor their deeper potentials. They see their children through a glass darkly because that is how they see themselves. Even loving parents often provide distorted mirroring, especially if they idealize or indulge their child. No matter how much our parents love us, they generally see *their version* of who we are, as reflected in the dark glass of their own hopes, fears, expectations, and unmet needs. This is not something to blame them for, because they probably never had much help recognizing or valuing their deeper nature either. They simply couldn't give us a kind of recognition they never gave themselves. Nor could they allow us to have feelings, needs, or sensitivities they never allowed themselves to have.

This is the tremendously challenging situation that every child must learn to deal with. Though as children we need adult mirroring to help us accept and relate to the whole range of our experience, we usually receive partial or distorted reflections, or else no reflection at all. And this brings up the most primal of fears—that there is something wrong with our experience, that we are in some way deficient, unworthy, or unacceptable, or that we don't really exist.

When the adult world—either through misunderstanding, neglect, or outright abuse—fails to see or value us as children, we feel deeply hurt. Our soul experiences a kind of shock, which closes down the natural openness of our being. Emily Dickinson described this in one of her poems:

> *There is a pain so utter*
> *It swallows Being up.*

For some of us, this pain is so intense or traumatic that it threatens to overwhelm us, disrupt our equilibrium, or blow the fuses in our delicate nervous system. So we learn to shut ourselves down, like a circuit breaker, or curl up in a ball and play dead. For others, this closing down may come about more gradually, as a result of not being fully seen or responded to over a long period of time.

Our basic state of openness, which often feels like a soft spot at the core of our being, is the source of love and many other essential human qualities. Yet it also gives rise to intense psychological pain in childhood when we are not seen or valued. In order to reduce our sensitivity to this pain, which threatens our equilibrium, we learn to shut down the openness of our body and mind. This gives us a sense of control, helping us adapt to and survive the vicissitudes of our family circumstances. The child is like an open hand that gradually starts to contract and close.

Although clenching the hand into a fist may be a fitting response to immediate threat, it would obviously be inappropriate to walk around that way for the rest of our life. Yet this is exactly what happens in our psyche! Our first response to emotional pain is to flinch, which is not a problem in and of itself. But then we start to take refuge in this contraction, and identify with it. It feels safer to be a closed fist than a vulnerable open hand. This protective tightening becomes installed in our body/mind as a set of chronic, rigid defenses that cut us off from our feelings and thus shut down our capacity to respond to life freely and openly. In our attempt to say no to the pain, we wind up saying no to ourselves instead. In this way, *we inflict on ourselves the core wound that will haunt us the rest of our lives: We start to separate from our own being.*

In shutting down like this, we also close off our access to inner resources that we need for handling life's challenges. By always trying to avoid feeling vulnerable, for instance, we never develop the very resource—genuine courage—that would help us handle our vulnerable feelings. Similarly, turning away from our pain diminishes our capacity for compassion, the most effective antidote to human suffering. As we lose access to these inner resources, we develop holes or "dead spots" in our psyche—places where we have gone numb, where the energy of awareness no longer circulates freely.

In this way, we close off, one by one, most of the rooms in the palace of our being. The palace keeps shrinking until one day we wake up to find ourselves living in a small, one-room flat. And so, for Hesse's hero Anselm, whose life was once filled with the magical delights of the garden, there comes a season unlike the others:

> Nothing was any longer the way it had always been. The boy was frequently at odds with his mother. He himself did not know what the trouble was or why it hurt so, why something was always bothering him. He only saw that the world had changed. The colored stones around the garden bored him, the flowers were silent, and he kept the beetles in a case, impaled on pins. The old joys had dried up and withered, and his soul had begun the long, hard detour.

False Self as Soul-Cage

The soul's long, hard detour begins in childhood as we close off the vast potentials of our being and take up residence in a tiny, one-room flat. This confining room is our ego or conditioned personality, which develops as a strategy for adapting to a world that does not seem to support who we really are. Our personality is a composite of various identities—fixed beliefs about ourselves—that defend us from threatening feelings.

As a way to defend against the fear that we are nobody, for example, we might try to see ourselves as big and tough. We tell ourselves, "This is who I am—someone who isn't afraid, someone who can handle anything." If we can't handle our grief or sadness, we might develop an identity as "a cheerful, optimistic person," someone who is above such feelings. Or if our need for love has been frustrated, we may construct a facade of pretending not to have any needs. Eventually we start to believe that we *really don't* need love. And such beliefs create a distorted picture of reality—which is like a waking dream or trance we come to live within. Emily Dickinson describes this whole sequence of events in eight precise lines:

> *There is a pain so utter*
> *It swallows Being up.*
> *Then covers the abyss with trance,*
> *So memory can step*
> *Around, across, upon it,*
> *As one within a swoon*
> *Goes steady, when an open eye*
> *Would drop him bone by bone.*

The abyss she speaks of here refers to the sense of inner emptiness that results from losing touch with our being. As children, we need to cover this abyss with trance—with beliefs, imaginings, and stories about who we are—to distract ourselves from this painful loss, so that our mind can "step around, across, upon it." The "somebody" we imagine ourselves to be is a false self that provides a semblance of security and control ("as one within a swoon goes steady"), where facing the loss of connection with our being would seem devastating ("when an open eye would drop him bone by bone"). Thus, at least some of the time, our false self functions as a cozy, comfortable cocoon where we feel safe.

Yet since it is made up of frozen, distorted images of ourselves, the false self is also a soul-cage, which prevents us from knowing who we really are or living freely and expansively. Our conditioned personality always contains a haunting sense of deficiency, a sense that we have somehow lost touch with our wholeness and depth, with the meaning and magic of life.

On the Razor's Edge

In the Hesse story, the time comes when Anselm starts to construct a false self to shield himself from the pain of his own loss of being. Adopting a bold and worldly air, he turns away from the magical garden of his youth where he once contemplated the peace and joy within his soul. He starts to live in his mind, eventually becoming a scholar and professor of great renown. Yet once he achieves this status, he also realizes that his life has become flat, stale, joyless.

This is what happens when we lose touch with our soul. To make up for our loss of being, we try to establish our value through having and doing: "I have, therefore I am. I do, therefore I am." This leaves us with a tremendous sense of emptiness and frustration; no matter how much we have or do, we still sense that something is missing. Eventually we imagine that finding someone to love will fill up our emptiness and set everything right.

Thus Anselm finds himself becoming fascinated by a delicate, beautiful woman by the name of Iris. Something about her seems strangely familiar, and she evokes feelings in him he is unable to name. Although drawn to her, he also has his doubts. She doesn't fit in with his professional life and worldly designs. And he senses that a relationship with her could wreak enormous changes in him—a prospect that both frightens and intrigues him.

When we start to fall in love, such mixed feelings are not unusual. The prospect of new possibilities, new beginnings, new worlds opening up causes our soul to expand. The doors of our one-room flat swing open and we feel excited about the possibility of reinhabiting the larger palace of our being. Yet something stops us at the threshold. There are no lights on in the neglected rooms and corridors of the palace. There are cobwebs in the corners and who knows what else? As we expand in love, we start to encounter closed-off parts of ourselves, with which we are not on friendly terms. This feels dangerous and threatening.

If I have shunned and denied my need for love, for instance, then when this need arises in a relationship, I won't know what to do with it—how to feel it, how to express it, how to handle it. It seems like a black hole that could engulf me and swallow me alive. What will happen to me if I acknowledge this need? Will I lose all my strength? Who will I be? My very survival appears to be at stake.

Standing on the threshold of this long-neglected part of myself, I feel raw and shaky. I'm not an expert here. As my conscious identity—my facade of self-sufficiency—is undermined, a deeper unconscious identity threatens to emerge. I fear that I will become like a dependent, needy child, at other people's mercy. Demons appear, trying to discourage me from crossing this threshold. "Get back!" they say. "You closed off that room for good reason. Do you really think you can handle what's in it? Watch out! You might really lose it if you go there!"

It's true: I might really "lose it." But that's what makes love so intriguing: Losing it—letting go of old, confining identities—is totally exciting *and* totally frightening. This makes for a most interesting situation. I am pulled in opposite directions: expanding and contracting, wanting to go forward and wanting to maintain my defenses at the same time.

This is why intimate relationship can be such a potent vehicle for wisdom and awakening. It allows us to experience both sides of our nature—the call of our larger being and the fear and insecurity of our false self—at once, right next to each other. On this threshold, where part of us wants to expand and part of us wants to pull back, we stand on a razor's edge—the boundary of the unknown, and the frontier of a whole new way of being.

Taking the Leap

Anselm decides to take the leap. He asks Iris to marry him. She responds without hesitation: "You offer me flowers, yet I can live without flowers and many other things as well. But one thing I cannot and will not do without: I can never live so much as a single day in which the music in my heart is not dominant. If I am to live with a man, it must be one whose inner music harmonizes with mine, and his single desire must be that his own music be pure."

Her response renders Anselm speechless, and he nervously crushes a flower in his hand. Then in the great tradition of romantic love, which calls the lover to heroic deeds, Iris lays down a further condition. If he wants her as his wife, he must go in search of what her name reminds him of. "You have lost and forgotten something important and holy, something that must be reawakened before you can find happiness. On the day when you have rediscovered that, I will go with you as your wife wherever you wish."

Iris is giving voice to love's most fundamental and insistent demand: You must change your life. You must live in harmony with the soul's inner music. You must find out who you really are and what you most deeply desire. You must awaken from your trance and find your way back to your home-ground, your true nature.

No task in Anselm's life had ever been so daunting. And while he has doubts about what Iris is asking of him, a voice inside him recognizes that she is right—"and it made the same demand that she did." Though Anselm had hoped that marrying Iris would provide the happiness he was lacking, he now realizes that their relationship is calling him to something deeper—reclaiming his soul.

And so he takes up her challenge. As he searches within himself for the forgotten mystery glimpsed in childhood, Anselm is forced to confront the painful truth about his life: He has become a dry, hollow shell. This acknowledgment is a first, essential step in reconnecting with his soul; for it is his soul that feels the pain of being confined in an empty shell. Out of this sorrow a new longing is born—to find himself.

Finding ourselves means freeing ourselves from the conditioned personality and becoming the authentic individual that we are called to be. (*Individual* literally means *undivided*—having access to the full range of our powers and potentials—instead of living divided against ourselves.) As Anselm sets out on this path, he starts to come back to life and respond more deeply to the world around him. People notice a new warmth and vitality in him. Finally he comes to realize that there is no turning back from the journey on which he has embarked.

Ripening Through Love

So it is for most of us. Love first arrives as a state of grace. But as it fills us and causes us to expand, it also brings us up against obstacles blocking that expansion—the bars of our soul-cage, all the ways we have turned away from our true nature and shriveled up inside. If, for example, we harbor an image of ourselves as unlovable, then when the opportunity arises to be loved for who we really are, we won't know how to handle it. Even though this is what we truly long for, it also frightens us to death, because it threatens our whole identity! To let love enter all the way into us, we have to give up who we think we are.

Love always presents this kind of challenge, because it requires letting go of old identities that have served as a protective shell. To love and be loved, the false self has to die. This is the death that the Sufi poet Ibn Al Faradh speaks of when he writes:

> *Death through love is life;*
> *I give thanks to my beloved that she*
> *has held it out for me.*
> *Whoever does not die of his love is*
> *unable to live by it.*

Like the sun's rays that cause the seed to stir within its husk, love's radiant energy penetrates the facade of the false self, calling forth resources hidden deep within us. Its warmth wakes up the life inside us, making us want to uncurl, to give birth, to grow and reach for the light. It calls on us to break out of our shell, the personality-husk surrounding the seed potential of all that we could be.

The purpose of a seed husk is to protect the tender life within until the time and conditions are right for it to burst forth. Our personality structure serves a similar function. It provides a semblance of security, as a kind of compensation for the loss of our larger being. But when love's warming rays start to wake us up, our ego-shell becomes a barrier restricting our expansion. As the germ of life swells within us, we feel our imprisonment more acutely.

The urge to break out of our dark shell also activates our demons, the voices of our fear, which urge us to stay safely ensconced behind the walls of our habitual defenses. In showing us the way out of our prison, love forces us to do battle with these demons, for they are our prison guards.

Since it is easy to start doubting ourselves when we encounter our darkness and demons, it is important to understand that a wholesome logic operates here: The brighter love's radiance, the darker the shadows we encounter; the more we feel life stirring within us, the more we also feel our dead spots; the more conscious we become, the more clearly we see where we remain unconscious. None of this need dishearten us. For in facing our darkness, we bring to light forgotten parts of our being. In recognizing exactly where we have been unconscious, we become more conscious. And in seeing and feeling the ways we've gone dead, we start to revive and kindle our desire to live more expansively.

True love always requires great daring. Although we might like to think of love only in terms of the light it brings into our life, if we are not also willing to confront the darkness that this light reveals, our soul will never ripen or evolve. As Hesse puts it, "The soul is rich, healthy, and capable of happiness only when there is a constant exchange, a mutual renewal, between the darkness and the field of light." Trying to avoid this polar tension at the core of our nature—between light and shadow, expansion and contraction—only impoverishes the soul.

Awareness born of love is the only force that can bring healing and renewal. Out of our love for another person, we become more willing to let our old identities wither and fall away, and enter a dark night of the soul, so that we may stand naked once more in the presence of the great mystery that lies at the core of our being. This is how love ripens us—by warming us from within, inspiring us to break out of our shell, and lighting our way through the dark passage to new birth.

DIALOGUE 2A

Being on the Edge

Note: This dialogue, as well as the others in the book, are taken from relationship workshops, using exercises that illustrate main ideas in the preceding chapter. Because the workshop participants have been working intensively with this material, as well as cultivating greater self-awareness through meditation practice, their understandings, insights, and experiential shifts are often accelerated, compared with typical couples therapy.

My wife, Jennifer, was a co-leader in many of these dialogues, but for the sake of clarity and simplicity, I have not singled out her input from my own. The participants' words are in italics, while ours appear in roman.

We can only respond to love's invitation to grow and expand when we are willing to let a relationship take us to our edge—that place where an old identity no longer serves us and something totally new can begin to emerge. This is one of the most creative moments in a relationship. If we are to remain alive and growing in a relationship, we have to learn to stay connected with ourselves when we encounter one of these edges.

To explore this experientially, you might consider some particular difficulty in your present relationship, in the last relationship you were in, or in relationships in general. Tune into your body and see how this particular difficulty feels. In paying attention to this feeling, ask yourself—letting the answer come from the feeling rather than from your mind—"What's the hardest thing about this? How does this get to me? What bothers me most about this?"

Then, still paying attention to how this difficulty feels, ask yourself, "What resource is this calling on me to draw forth from within myself?" Or, "What do I need to cultivate to be able to face and work with this difficulty?" Don't answer the question with your mind. Feel it out and see what comes to you. What is it like to see this difficulty as an opportunity to develop this important resource?

KATE

A lot's going on inside, as though my whole body is vibrating. The difficulty I looked at was my fear of not being really valued and loved in a relationship. And I realized that this was calling on me to develop inner strength. As I acknowledged that, there was a sense of exhilaration, a rush of energy into the places in my body where I was feeling the pain of the difficulty.

So when you recognized that your fear of not being loved is calling on you to develop a certain kind of inner strength, you experienced an energy rush.

The energy seemed to be going into all those places where I felt tight, and opening them up. Then all of a sudden there was more space, and I felt more like myself. I sensed new possibilities. I felt powerful, like, "Oh, I can handle this."

A sense of opening up, expansion, power, and—

A big "Aha."

That's what can happen on the razor's edge. When you're on the threshold of an unexplored area in your palace, you may feel shaky at first, but as you move across the threshold, you sense an expansion because that palace is so large. And that's exhilarating.

When I felt the difficulty itself, I sensed a constriction in my chest. Then when I felt what it was calling on me to develop, that was just the opposite: a kind of opening.

In the difficulty, you felt constricted. But when you realized what it was calling you toward, something started to open. So you experienced yourself both contracting and expanding. That's how you know you're on the razor's edge. There's some resistance, because you're leaving your old comfort zone and entering unknown territory. But there's also some excitement: "Oh this could take me to a new place, somewhere I really need to go." That's what it's like to discover a path opening up before us.

In coming to this threshold, the edge of the unknown, which is scary and exciting at the same time, we start to find a path—a new direction, a way forward.

I also had a strong sense of how intimate it would be to share this experience with another person, how it would be bonding in an incredibly deep way.

That's exactly the point.

ROY

My main difficulty in my marriage has been my fear of sharing my real feelings with my partner—which often keeps us from being close or intimate. This is like a Zen koan for me. It forces me to look at how I go about my whole life. I usually take pride in handling things in a competent way, but I recognize this is also a trap. Having to be so competent makes it hard to feel what is going on inside me and to be fully present with my wife. I can go for weeks without being in touch with my feelings, without knowing what they are—and without even knowing that I don't know.

If I pay attention to my feelings, I'm afraid I won't be in control of what happens, where they will lead. I equate knowing the next step with rightness, with value, with success, with virtue or strength—all the things I'm supposed to have in this life. But though I've been a great success at being competent, I've created a solid wall between me and my feelings, and a perfect rationale for not needing to look over that wall.

How does all of this feel to you right now?

It's very sad.

Can you sense that sadness in your body right now? What's most sad about this for you?

What's sad is how trapped I am behind that wall of competence, how cut off I am from what I feel.

What's it like to acknowledge this sadness?

It seems sort of hopeless. I don't know what to do with this. I guess I'm pitting my need to be competent against letting myself feel the sadness. That's what I always do, and the score is 100 to nothing.

So even acknowledging your sadness about being cut off activates your usual coping strategy—trying to be competent and in charge. It seems hopeless because you imagine, "If I let myself feel this sadness, I won't be in control." Since you always choose competence over feeling, the score is: ego, 100, soul, 0. But this sadness itself is arising from your soul. The sadness is saying, "Wait a minute, there's a whole part of me that's been totally neglected and left out."

Instead of seeing your sadness as something you have to cope with in some competent way, you might recognize it as a call. Some part of yourself is calling out to you, "I've been neglected." Acknowledging that might provide an opportunity to even the score.

I feel like I'm walking along a wall, a very long wall, and I can't see what's on the other side.

That sounds like the razor's edge.

There are a few peepholes I can look through, but I don't allow myself to look through them very often. That's very sad.

Two things are happening right now. You're contracting—judging yourself for not seeing through that wall. But something else is also happening, something softer and more expansive: You're acknowledging how painful your situation is and letting that touch you.

That brings back the sadness.

Yes, so can you let the sadness just be there?

Yes, I can now. That's a big relief. It feels . . . clearing. But it's quickly followed by the depressing thought, "Oh, God, I've really got a lot of work to do." Or, "I'm really not so competent after all."

Right. So there you are again—both expanding and contracting. As soon as you step over the threshold into new territory, these old stories come up that push you back into the habitual pattern. They arise from the old identity that's trying to keep you in its grip—Roy the Competent. The old identity is trying to scare you by saying, "Hey, don't let go of *me*, the competent one. Because if you let go of *me*, who knows what will happen?"

It feels like a fear of death. The old identity doesn't want to die.

Of course. You've put a lot of psychic energy into this identity. It's become a fixation that doesn't want to let go.

If I let it go, I'm afraid I would have feelings that I couldn't tolerate.

Yes, you're afraid you won't be able to handle your feelings. But you don't know for sure. That's only a guess.

An educated guess.

As a child it was probably true that you couldn't handle them. But as an adult you've never really given them a chance. You've never learned to open to the feelings you're so afraid of. So the truth is, you don't really know if you could handle them or not. But the scare story that comes up for you on this edge is, "I'd better not look over the wall because there may be a monster on the other side." If you keep buying into that story, it will keep you stuck on this side of the wall forever.

Let me ask you this: What is your fear of your feelings calling on you to find or cultivate in yourself?

When you ask that, I sense a choking in my throat. I have never asked myself that in my whole life. It feels really profound. As I consider this, I realize I am being called on to love and accept myself, and not make myself wrong. To have compassion and not be afraid of loss. That touches me very deeply.

Good. That's powerful.

It's calling on me to do an awful lot.

Yes. It's like seeing your whole life's work laid out in front of you.

It's hard when your parents never gave you much acceptance or support. Sometimes it seems like an overwhelming task—almost like preparing for a mountaineering expedition.

Yes, sometimes it's hard to feel your feelings. But be careful about making it into a task or obligation, something you have to push yourself to accomplish. That will throw you back into your competent mode and keep you stuck.

It might be more helpful to see this as an exploration, a journey to a new land. That's why I recommend just sitting on the edge, and then seeing what arises naturally, seeing what beckons to you there. There's no need to push yourself over the edge. It's better to let your desire for what's on the other side of that wall build gradually, of its own accord.

I can see that some relaxation and gentleness are needed here.

So cultivating gentleness also becomes an important part of your path. Without some gentleness, warmth, and compassion, there's not going to be much growth.

When we're on an edge, we often feel both a desire to expand into new territory and a fear of that. Being gentle here means acknowledging both sides of what you're feeling, instead of pushing yourself forward or scaring yourself into pulling back. That will help you relax, stay present, and see what wants to happen next.

That's good. That helps me focus right on where I need to be.

ELIZABETH

My big difficulty in relationships is feeling overly dependent on my partner.

What's hardest about that for you?

I start to become afraid I'll be abandoned. When I get in touch with that, it feels awesome and I can't seem to go any further. As soon as I get close to this fear of abandonment, I suddenly fade and go blank.

What do you need to draw on in yourself in order to be here with this fear?

I don't know. I can't get past this.

Get past what? What are you trying to get past?

My fear of abandonment.

You're trying to get *past* it—*that's* the problem. The truth is, you don't know how to deal with this fear of abandonment. It brings you to the razor's edge. Not feeling sure of what to do is what it feels like to be on this edge.

So it's okay not to know what to do with this fear. You don't have to get past it. This is a doorway for you. If you can just sit there on the threshold and be with your experience, something might open up. What's it feel like right now?

I'm going blank.

What's making you go blank? Is it because you don't want to experience what's going on here? Do you see any value in working with this or—

Yes, I definitely do. I just can't seem to . . . I mean . . .

Let's see what is making you go blank.

It's rage.

Rage. Okay. What in the rage needs your attention?

Sadness.

So underneath the rage is sadness. What in the sadness needs your attention and caring?

I'm fading out again.

That's okay. You don't have to push through this. You start to approach your edge, and then you back off when it starts to feel threatening. That's okay. The point is to be present with whatever goes on for you here on this edge. This is a very fertile place for you. Do you have a sense of that?

Oh, very much.

So approach it gently. You could start by being gentle with your feelings. That will open up some space around them, and help you be with them. You don't have to sail right through them to get somewhere else. What's important is just to allow this sadness and contact yourself there.

Yes. I can do that. That feels better. I usually go into panic when I feel this and then go blank.

Going blank is a way of cutting yourself off from a feeling that seems threatening, that brings you to an edge where you don't know what to do.

But you're on the right track here. You were able to acknowledge your fear of abandonment, as well as your tendency to run away or go blank when you encounter it. Underneath the fear you discovered rage, and recognizing that led you to some sadness, which you acknowledged as well. In this way, you're learning to remain present on your edge. How do you feel right now?

I feel better now seeing all of this.

As you connect with the feelings that come up when you acknowledge your fear of abandonment, you actually start to heal that abandonment wound, because you're there for yourself in a new way. You're no longer abandoning yourself.

Chapter Three

Up Against the Walls

You have always been free!
Do not be fooled by the I and the Other.

SARAHA

Even couples who share a vision of relationship as an opportunity for personal or spiritual development often find it hard to put this vision into practice—to regard the difficulties in their way as creative challenges rather than intractable problems. Why is it that even when two partners have a strong connection and the best of intentions, their relationship still sometimes leaves them feeling trapped and desperate, threatened and overwhelmed?

What usually makes couples feel most stuck are repetitive conflicts that go nowhere, continually leading to the same lack of communication and understanding. The same impasse comes up again and again, triggering a fruitless round of argument and counterargument, action and reaction, attack and withdrawal. The Eastern traditions have a word for these recurring cycles of frustration that ensnare us—*samsara*. In Western terms, we might simply call them *hell*, as when people claim that "marriage is hell."

While most couples would agree that such recurring struggles are fruitless, they keep repeating them just the same. Why do lovers find it so hard to remain in the bright, dynamic presence that first attracted them to each other? Why do they act and react in ways that create so much suffering instead?

When caught in the middle of a conflict with our partner, we might be tempted to answer this question by agreeing with the character in a Sartre play who declares that "Hell is other people." Yet it would be much more accurate to say, "Hell is *how we see ourselves in relation to other people*." Relationship conflict becomes a hellish struggle or deadlock when it re-evokes and snags us in some constricting identity from the past that is associated with profound psychic pain. And the conflict can go nowhere as long as we continue playing it out with our partner instead of addressing its source—the negative view of ourselves that has been activated, and that is undermining our basic sense of existence, validity, or worth.

Unconscious Identities

Douglas was an intelligent, creative man who consistently had trouble handling women's anger. Whenever his partner would express any anger, he would react with righteous indignation, telling himself, "I don't need this in my life." This reaction arose from his view of himself as a spiritual person, someone who would never stoop to such crude emotions.

Douglas had begun to develop this sense of detachment in childhood, as a way to shield himself from the ugly, ferocious fights that took place between his parents. But this was only a facade covering up a secret belief that he was someone who could easily be crushed by other people's anger. His partner's anger threatened him because it re-evoked a painful sense of himself as a victim—someone who felt small and inadequate. This was not how Douglas wanted to see himself or be seen by others. So his defensive strategy was to gain the upper hand by taking the high road, adopting a "superior" spiritual stance in an attempt to avoid conflict with other people.

Our ego or conditioned personality is composed of various identifications, or self-images, and develops in childhood as a form of self-protection. It begins as an attempt to cover over and compensate for our loss of being, by fabricating certain qualities that we need, but that seem to be missing. For example, if we did not receive the kind of support that would have nurtured our inner strength, we might *try* to be strong through force of will: "I'll be strong. I won't let this bother me. I'll overcome this. . . ." This attempt to make ourselves strong forms a *conscious* identity—an image of ourselves that we promote and defend in order to cover up an inner sense of lack. Underneath our conscious identity is an *unconscious* identity, our identification with that lack; in this case, our secret belief that we are not really strong, but weak instead. We construct a conscious identity—a facade or "cover story"—to ward off and shield us from this more painful, threatening unconscious identity.

Thus our ego structure serves a useful function in childhood. As an attempt to supply what is missing, it protects us from having to feel the pain of our losses. For example, our fabricated strength, which we activate by tensing our muscles or gritting our teeth, may help us to endure and survive difficult circumstances; and this keeps us from having to experience our lack of true inner strength. But later in life, especially in intimate relationships, this facade becomes a hindrance, for it is a false self that prevents us from being genuine with our partner. It also keeps us from discovering our true strength, which can never be fabricated, but only discovered as an intrinsic quality of our very being.

The ego's agenda in relationships is to have other people confirm our conscious identity. If our partner sees us as strong, for instance, that will validate our self-image as a strong person, and help us ward off the more terrifying belief that we are really weak instead. So our *hope* is that our conscious identity will be confirmed, and our *fear* is that our unconscious identity will be revealed and exposed for all to see. This dynamic of hope and fear is what keeps the whirlwind of samsara, or confusion, in relationships spinning round and round.

With Douglas, whenever his partner became angry, this threatened to expose his unconscious identity as a small, defenseless child, hidden behind his facade as a highly evolved spiritual being. His defense was to treat his partner in a righteous, scornful way. Yet his cold disdain only triggered one of *her* most painful unconscious identities—as someone unworthy of love—and this intensified her wrath. For Douglas, seeing and feeling himself as prey to other people's anger felt, literally, like hell; for his partner, hell was seeing and feeling herself as unworthy of love. In reacting against their own internal hells, they each triggered the other's hell-state—which led to a recurring pattern of conflict that seemed impossible to resolve.

If relationship conflicts did not snag us in this way— by exposing unconscious identities we have spent our whole life trying to ward off—they would simply arise, be worked with, and pass away. For instance, even if my partner and I often felt angry with each other, this would not be a problem as long as we could move nimbly through these feelings. Then the anger would just be energy, like a passing storm, and might even intensify our passion, generate humor, bring attention to issues that need to be addressed, or energize our communication.

But as soon as my partner's anger stirs up one of my unconscious identities, the problems begin. I no longer respond flexibly to the situation at hand. It's as though I fall into a trance, in which I am watching an old movie playing in my mind, rather than seeing and responding to what is actually happening. Perhaps her anger makes me feel like a helpless child. In my trance state, I may see myself as a bad boy being scolded by his mother.

This view of myself is so painful and threatening that I feel compelled to ward it off. Up comes a defensive facade: I try to show my partner that I am really tough, perhaps by lashing out at her and making her feel bad instead. But reacting in this defensive way leads nowhere. It distances me from myself, by denying what is *really* going on inside me. And it distances me from my partner, further reinforcing my sense of being bad. All of this—the reaction to my partner as though she were my mother, the anger and defensiveness, and the loss of real connection with myself and with her—stems from the trance I fall into when this old, unconscious identity becomes activated. It all happens automatically, without much awareness of what is really going on.

Stuck in a Cage

Love's expansiveness inevitably brings us up against the walls of our personality structure, the prison of our old identities. Just as a prisoner who wants to escape from jail must carefully study its layout, we need to understand more precisely what these soul-cages are made of, if we want to free ourselves from them. This kind of self-inquiry is essential in making a relationship more conscious.

According to certain schools of modern psychology, our ego identities—the ways we see ourselves—originally develop out of our relations with others. Because we are born so totally open, we are easily affected and shaped by our impressions of how other people see us, treat us, respond to us. If the basic sensitivity of our nature is like soft wax, the impressions we take in as children are like imprints in this wax. As our mind fixates on these impressions, it's as if the surface of the wax starts to harden, and these impressions become etched into our psyche.

When we are young, our parents reflect back to us certain pictures of who we are *in their eyes*. Lacking our own self-reflective awareness, we inevitably start to internalize these reflections, coming to see ourselves in terms of how we appear to others. This is akin to looking at ourselves in a mirror and then taking that visual image, rather than our immediate, lived experience of embodied presence, to be who we are. The mirror image provides a picture of how we appear to others. Yet because it also forces us to relate to ourselves as though from the position of an external observer, it separates us from our direct sense of ourselves as a living being. When seeing ourselves in terms of an image, we treat ourselves as an object. We become *an object of our thought*, rather than *the subject of our experience*. And this prevents us from knowing ourselves in a more direct, immediate way.

To form an identity means *taking ourselves to be something*, based on imagining that how others treat us means something about who we really are. For instance, a little boy whose father is always critical might take himself to be an inadequate person. It is only a small leap from "I can't seem to make my father happy," to "I must be an inadequate person," or from "My parents disapprove of me, and I feel bad," to "I must be bad," or to "I don't care what other people think—I'm better than they are anyway."

The problem here is that we take the reflections of ourselves in others' eyes to represent who we are, whether we like them or not. If we like them, they become woven into a conscious identity that we promote and defend; if we don't like them, they become woven into an unconscious identity that we ward off. In either case, we fixate on these images, giving them more weight and credence than our own direct experience of ourselves. This makes them into soul-cages. Incorporating these self/other transactions into the core of our ego-identity, we grow up seeing ourselves in ways that separate us from our true nature and its full range of powers and potentials.

Self/Other Setups

We could describe these internalized self/other transactions as "interpersonal imprints" or "self/Other setups." (By *Other* with a capital "O," I mean the general sense of not-self that we carry inside us, while *other* with a small "o" refers to another individual.) Every self/Other setup consists of three elements: a view of Other, a view of self in relation to Other, and a feeling that accompanies this particular relation. If we see our parents as caring and supportive, we may develop a view of ourselves as worthwhile, and the corresponding feeling might be confidence or self-respect. If our parents are abusive, we may come to see Other as threatening and ourselves as a victim; and our life may be permeated by a mood of fear, distrust, or paranoia. Every view of Other implies a view of self, and every view of self implies a view of Other.

These self/Other imprints we carry within us operate like unconscious templates determining how we set up our relationships. Sometimes their influence is obvious, as when a woman who was criticized by her father repeatedly chooses critical men; seeing herself as unworthy, she may look for a partner who devalues her *because that is what she knows, that is her unconscious sense of reality*. These setups may also affect couples in more subtle, less apparent ways, and may be harder to detect if several different, even contradictory patterns are operating at the same time.

Yet in one way or another, two partners usually act out some form of matching identities, especially in the early phases of their relationship. Whatever part we are playing, we unconsciously tend to look for or create the corresponding role in our partner. Even when those we love don't entirely match our inner templates, we tend to focus on and bring out the parts of them that do.

For example, a woman whose father abandoned the family when she was young believed that men could never really be there for her. Whenever her partner wasn't totally available and loving, she would feel anxious and start a fight. In effect, she fell into a trance where she saw her partner as an abandoning parent whose actions were saying, "I don't care about you. You're not important." And this in turn brought up an unconscious identity she had hoped that love would save her from: seeing herself as worthless.

In truth, her partner *was* potentially there for her. But when she was in her trance she could only see the twenty percent of him that wasn't there, instead of the eighty percent that was. Pushing him away with her attacks actually reinforced the unavailable part of him. The more she acted out her inner setup, the more it became a self-fulfilling prophecy, keeping them both stuck in fruitless, repetitive conflict.

In this way, identities generate faulty perceptions of reality—trance states—that cause us to perceive and respond to those we love in distorted ways. And they will continue to operate like this *until we start bringing them into the light of consciousness*. Relationships call forth this kind of heightened awareness by showing us exactly how and where we are stuck. Instead of seeing our partner as our jailer, we need to see that we have constructed our own cage, one we have been carrying around a long time, and that we alone keep ourselves confined there.

Mutual Liberation

Since we originally lost touch with ourselves in our relations with others, that is where we often seek to find ourselves again. In truth, a good relationship *can* help us become more whole, but not in the magical way we often imagine. Instead, by calling forth deeper qualities of our nature that we have lost touch with, love also brings us up against confining identities that normally cut off our access to these qualities. And this provides a special opportunity: We have to be pushed right up against our prison walls—which are made out of old self-images—before we can start to break through them and discover who we really are. Once we are up against these walls, the need for a conscious relationship becomes more apparent, and also more imperative.

Jill was a classic "woman who loved too much," who had spent three years trying to work out a relationship with a man who withheld his love from her. Even though Terry provided little in the way of emotional availability or commitment, she kept hoping he would finally come around, see the light, and open up to her at last. All these years her main focus had been on Terry: what he gave her and what he didn't give her. If only Terry would love her, she imagined she would be magically healed. Then at last she would feel whole and at ease.

Jill had been extremely close to an older brother when she was young, sharing with him a loving connection that she lacked with her parents. However, in later years when he came home from college, he would mostly ignore her, while she kept trying to win a few crumbs of affection from him. This bittersweet relationship reinforced an earlier setup with her father, where she saw herself as small and unlovable, and Other as all-powerful and remote. Although she longed to win over a man and have him recognize her beauty, her inner setup made her choose men who rebuffed her.

What kept Jill's hope alive with Terry were times when the ache of her longing became so intense that her heart would break open and temporarily sweep away all her fear and insecurity. In these moments she became so lucid, present, and sweet that he could no longer resist her, and would briefly open up to her. These breakthroughs, though fleeting, strengthened her resolve to hang in there with him.

The situation only began to change when Jill realized that she was acting out with Terry what was essentially an inner drama. Having internalized the rejecting attitudes of her father and brother, she had grown up regarding her softer, feminine qualities as a deficiency. Only in occasional moments of closeness with her brother, when she temporarily won his affection, had she been able to appreciate herself fully. And so when her heart would break open with Terry and her sweetness overflowed, she experienced what it was like to be fully present, fully herself once more. Gradually Jill began to realize that what she really wanted was her own wholeness, which she could have only by embracing all of herself, rather than chasing madly after Terry—which only kept her trapped in an old identity. As she learned to give herself the deeper recognition she needed, her compulsion to win him over began to diminish.

Until this point, Jill's enslavement by an unconscious identity—as someone who only deserved crumbs—had allowed Terry to keep hiding out in his conscious identity—as someone who was too good to have to attend to others' needs. He maintained this stance as a defense against a much more threatening, unconscious self-image—where he saw himself a slave to others' expectations. As the oldest of five boys, Terry had come to believe that he had to hold the family together by doing his mother's bidding, or else she and the whole family would fall apart. Given this constricting sense of duty, the main way he had found to feel free and powerful was through refusing to give himself to a woman. When Jill would act like a "slave of love," this allowed Terry to avoid feeling his own inner sense of bondage.

As Jill woke up from the trance created by her deficient self-image, and withdrew her fixation on Terry, he could no longer maintain his old position of power. This forced him to feel his own inner sense of deficiency, which he had been avoiding by letting Jill carry it for him. Though he was angry about this, he eventually began to respect her in a new way. Somewhere deep within he recognized the changing situation as an opportunity to face his own demons and loosen the inner shackles that kept his soul imprisoned. In this way, Jill's work on freeing herself helped to free Terry as well. Though they still had a long way to go, they were finally starting to see each other as real human beings.

Even in the best of relationships, two people's unconscious setups inevitably create a mutual entanglement that causes them both suffering. Yet this suffering is also a call to wake up from the mistaken identities in which they are trapped. Some couples fail to recognize this call or reject it outright, succumbing to the entanglement instead. Others simply end the relationship. Not realizing that their own conditioned patterns form their prison, they see their partner as their jailer, someone who prevents them from feeling alive and free.

If a couple can respond to the call to wake up from their mutual trance, they can become powerful allies. Any step either of them takes will help the other. When one of them is no longer willing to play out an old identity, such as victim or pursuer, the other can no longer maintain the matching identity, as oppressor or distancer. In bringing greater consciousness to these setups, two partners help each other loosen their attachment to the false self, so that they can begin relating to each other more fully in the present moment, as who they really are.

Dialogue 3A

Recognizing Unconscious Setups

One way to start uncovering unconscious setups operating in your relationships is to examine a recurring conflict or problem with your partner or a former partner. What is the picture you hold of the other person and how he or she contributes to the problem? Then look at the image of yourself that goes along with your image of the other person. How do you see yourself in this conflict? That will give you the two ends of the setup operating here: the view of Other and the view of self.

Next you might notice how these two pictures match and fit together. What does this setup remind you of from your past?

What feeling comes up when you look at this setup? How do you relate to this feeling? What do you do with it? Do you accept it? Or do you judge it or try to get rid of it? Can you give this feeling some space and let yourself experience it? What is that like?

If you can open to the feelings that come up when you bring an old identity into consciousness, this will help loosen the hold of the identity, which originally formed as a reaction against these very feelings.

BARRY

I'm always struggling to make my partner see my value. Somehow I'm never satisfied that she does, and I wind up feeling rejected by her.

So what is your view of Other in this situation?

I see her as a critical person.

43

And how do you see yourself in this struggle?

I see myself as not worthy of her understanding.

Does this remind you of anything from your past?

It reminds me of how my parents weren't supportive of me.

And what feeling goes along with this view of yourself?

Loneliness and emptiness.

In the self/Other setup operating here, you see your partner as critical and yourself as unworthy. And your struggle involves trying to get her to validate you, so you can feel your own value. When you recognize this, it brings up feelings of loneliness and emptiness. Those are the feelings that go along with seeing yourself as unworthy.

How do you relate to those feelings?

Painfully.

What do you do with them?

I try to get my partner to make me feel better, and when she doesn't, I withdraw into my cocoon. It's much safer in there because I don't feel that pain.

So you turn away from your pain.

You mentioned that your parents were unsupportive, so they must have dismissed your feelings. You probably felt rejected and concluded that you were unworthy. Now you carry this sense of rejection inside you. And you try to counteract this by getting your partner to validate you. When that doesn't work, it leaves you with a sense of loneliness and emptiness. But since you're afraid of those feelings, you reject them. And that puts you right back at square one—feeling rejected. That's how these setups work: You unconsciously keep re-creating the very rejection that you want to avoid.

I'm not clear how withdrawing into my cocoon re-creates the rejection, because it actually feels safer there.

When you turn away from your sense of loneliness and emptiness, you dismiss your present experience. You say, in effect, "I don't want my experience." And in cutting off these feelings, you reenact inside yourself the same lack of acceptance you originally felt from your parents. That keeps you stuck in an old identity where you feel unworthy and rejected.

The way to break out of this pattern is by letting yourself feel this loneliness and emptiness you've been running from all your life. If we can open to our experience just as it is, our inner contractions relax. This is the first step in freeing ourselves from an old setup that keeps making us feel bad about ourselves.

Often I don't accept my feelings because I'm afraid of wallowing in them or getting stuck in them.

That's probably what happened to you as a child—you *did* get stuck in them because you didn't know how to handle them. You closed off parts of your experience in order to keep your equilibrium. Unfortunately, that left a hole inside that you try to get your partner to fill.

What you can recognize now, as an adult, is that you have many more resources than you did as a child. You can discover that it's possible to experience the old empty feeling without being harmed by it. The only way to find that out is by remaining present with this feeling, without buying into any scare stories that your mind may fabricate.

I'm afraid that if I really feel my loneliness, I might get so angry that I'd attack the person who's rejecting me.

That's one of the scare stories that comes up on that edge. And if you believe it, it provides a reason to avoid the feeling. What would it be like instead to let the lonely feeling just be there instead?

It's uncomfortable to hang in with that feeling. That's why I push it away. But then I demand love in a manipulative way, so I don't have to feel that pain.

Yes. And what's different right now is that you're acknowledging all of that.

It's sad to realize I'm doing the same thing to myself that hurt so bad when I was growing up.

Can you open to that sadness?

Yes.

What's it like when you do that?

I feel some compassion for myself.

So when you open to your experience, something starts to soften. Do you feel that?

Yes. I feel more present.

Directly connecting with your experience activates awareness, courage, and compassion, the qualities most needed to melt down your old setup, with its double fixation—on self as unworthy and Other as critical. And that brings you back to who you are in the present moment. Trying to get your partner to accept you, on the other hand, only reinforces the double fixation, and the old setup.

TONY

The issue that came up for me is the pain I feel when my wife constantly tells me that I could be doing something better. The image I have of myself is Prometheus bound to a rock, with a vulture eating at my liver.

46

In this situation you see yourself as a victim and your wife as a predator. And how you feel in this setup is bound, helpless, hemmed in.

Hemmed in, right—not able to do anything except lash out at her.

How do you relate to that hemmed-in feeling?

I think I should escape or do something different.

A story comes up: "This shouldn't be happening to me." But how do you actually relate to the hemmed-in feeling?

I lash out.

That's how you *react against* feeling hemmed in. What is it like to experience the hemmed-in feeling itself?

I get apathetic.

That's another reaction. One reaction is to act out your frustration by lashing out, and the other is to cut off your feeling and go numb, right?

Right, essentially go numb.

"If I go numb, I won't have to feel anything. I won't stay bound to this rock with this vulture picking at my liver." Right?

Right.

But neither of those reactions does much for you. Instead, we need to look more carefully at what is happening for you when you feel bound like this.

I don't like it. I want to get rid of it. It makes me feel small, weak, powerless. It reminds me of how I felt stuck as a child and couldn't do anything other than feel frustrated.

No doubt feeling stuck like that was so painful that you warded off those powerless feelings as a child. But any part of our experience we reject eventually solidifies and turns into an unconscious identity. So what was once just a feeling—powerlessness—has now become a threatening self-image: seeing yourself as paralyzed, especially when your wife is critical. As long as you subconsciously see yourself that way, you will continue to be haunted by feelings of powerlessness.

The other option is to go to the edge of this black hole—this threatening feeling you've rejected—and see if you can be present there.

It's hard to imagine how to do that, what one does.

You don't have to *do* anything.

Well, it's hard to imagine how to not do *anything.*

Right, how not to react. It's difficult at first to face feelings you've been reacting against all your life. It might help to see them as belonging to the child, seeing the young boy in you who is struggling with something that seems so much bigger than him. How would you relate to a young child who was feeling that way?

I can feel for him.

Some compassion arises. Good. That is what will help you stay present with the powerless feeling.

Yes, I feel more able to be with this right now.

In learning to stand in the presence of the powerless feeling, you start to bring your adult consciousness to bear on that old identity frozen in time, where you see yourself as a small, helpless child. Then, instead of continuing to fixate on, and identify with, that image, you start to tap into certain inner resources—like presence, compassion, or courage—that will help you free yourself from its hold on you.

Chapter Four

SOULWORK AND
SACRED COMBAT

*It is with the soul that we grasp the essence of
another human being, not with the mind, nor even
with the heart.*

HENRY MILLER

*Do not believe that the battle of love is like other
fights. Its arrows and blows are gifts and blessings.*

FRANCISCO DE OSSUNA

Two kinds of deep affinity are essential for a conscious relationship. The first is a *heart connection*—that quality of pure, open presence, being to being—which we experience most vividly when we are in love. A reliable indicator of a heart connection is the sense of warmth and nourishing fullness that we feel in another person's presence.

A heart connection is a universal kind of love, which we can experience with anyone we feel open to, even a passing stranger. Yet it does not account for the special attraction we feel toward certain individuals with whom we sense a deep, unnameable resonance. This is the sign of another type of affinity, which we might call a *soul connection*.

Soul Connection and Soul

A soul connection is a resonance between two people who respond to the essential beauty of each other's individual natures, behind their facades, and who connect on this deeper level. This kind of mutual recognition provides the catalyst for a potent alchemy. It is a sacred alliance whose purpose is to help both partners discover and realize their deepest potentials. While a heart connection lets us appreciate those we love just as they are, a soul connection opens up a further dimension—seeing and loving them for *who they could be,* and for *who we could become under their influence.* This means recognizing that we both have an important part to play in helping each other become more fully who we are.

Someone who loves us can often see our soul potential more clearly than we can ourselves. When this happens, it has a catalytic effect; it invites and encourages dormant, undeveloped parts of us to come forth and find expression. Indeed, we are often most strongly attracted to those who we sense "will make us live—and die—most intensely . . . Sister souls recognize each other," as the French writer Suzanne Lilar points out. A soul connection not only inspires us to expand, but also forces us to confront whatever stands in the way of that expansion.

Soul, as I am using this term here, is not meant to indicate some metaphysical entity mysteriously inhabiting the body, but the unique, individual way that our larger being manifests in us, through us, *as us. Soul* is a way of speaking about the human element in us—that living sensitivity flowing deep within, often felt as a fluid yet definite sense of *being oneself,* a sense of inwardness, poignancy, or depth. In the words of the Sufi poet Rumi, soul is "a joy when kindness comes, a weeping at injury, a growing consciousness."

Whenever we see ourselves in terms of some fixed identity—"I am a happy person . . . a sad person . . . a spiritual seeker . . . a survivor"—we experience ourselves indirectly, through a self-concept. This is the false self—a mental construct or image of ourselves based on past experience. But in moments when we are in touch with soul, we experience ourselves freshly and immediately—as *this* being who is alive in *this* moment. This is our *true* individuality, our particular way of being, which allows us to connect with another person's particularity as well. When our heart is open, we can love anyone equally; yet when our soul is engaged, we love *this* person in a way that we love no other. When lovers meet on this level, their old identities fade into the background, and they become more energetically present, as I and Thou.

While our soul unfolds and reveals itself in uniquely personal ways, its roots extend much deeper than the personal realm. Like a separate drop of water with an innate tendency to find its way back to the ocean that is its source, soul contains a longing to connect with our home-ground, to realize our deeper essence as pure, open presence. Yet soul also contains a yearning to embody our larger nature *in this world,* to know ourselves *in this human form.* Thus soul is an intermediate principle or bridge, which allows a living integration between the two sides of our nature: the individual and the universal, the embodied realm of personal experience and the formless presence of pure being, pure spirit.

The experience of soul always contains this double yearning: to feel the meaning and beauty of our individual life, and to connect with the larger, universal currents of life flowing through us. As Rumi describes this two-way flow: "Do not think that the drop only becomes the ocean. The ocean too becomes the drop." If soul could describe itself, it would no doubt use words like those of Yunus Emre, another Sufi poet: "I am the drop that contains the sea. How beautiful to be an ocean hidden within an infinite drop."

Our great challenge as human beings is to live fully in both these worlds. We are not *just* this body/mind organism; we are also a being/awareness/presence much larger than our particular shape and form. Nor are we *just* this larger, formless being; we are also incarnate as this individual. If we identify totally with our form—our body/mind/personality—our life will remain confined within known, familiar structures. But if we try to live only as the formless, as pure spirit, we may find it hard to be grounded or engaged with our life. As a bridge between these two realms, soul makes itself felt through inner pulls and promptings, like a magnetic compass needle pointing the way, or a dowsing rod leading to water. When we become submerged in our ego-trance, it calls us to wake up; and if we try to float above this life, it calls us back to earth.

The Indian Tantric tradition sees the relationship between spirit and soul, between formless, absolute being and embodied, relative existence, as a play of lovers. As the Indian poet Tagore describes this play:

> The infinite seeks the intimate presence of the finite,
> the finite to disappear in the infinite.
> I do not know whose scheme this is . . .
> that the bound should be on a search after freedom—
> freedom asking to be housed in the bound.

While our absolute nature, as pure being or open presence, is timeless and changeless—"as it was in the beginning, is now, and ever shall be"—our soul evolves and deepens through cultivating and embodying the seed potentials—for courage, strength, generosity, humor, tenderness, wisdom—contained in this larger nature. The essence of spiritual work is to realize and continually reorient ourselves toward our being, our absolute nature; and this is what leads to ultimate freedom. Yet spiritual realizations often remain compartmentalized, apart from everyday life, or become used as a rationale for living in an impersonal and soulless way. That is why, if we are to *live* our realizations and bring them into this world, we also need to work on the *vessel* of spirit—our embodied humanity. Soulwork is the forging of this vessel. It involves breaking open the husks of the conditioned identities that encase our seed potentials, as well as plowing and cultivating the soil of our deeper humanness, so that these seeds can blossom and bear fruit.

This kind of cultivation takes patience, dedication, and perseverance—which is why Rilke once described the soulwork of relationship as "day labor, day labor, God knows there is no other word for it." It involves working with the contradictions of being human, and through that, developing our capacity to span these contradictions. Our true individuality will not unfold, nor will we be able to create a deep, transformative relationship in our lives, if we recognize only one side of our nature—either disregarding our personal experience, or else totally identifying with it. If spiritual work brings freedom, soulwork brings integration. Both are necessary for a complete human life.

The more we bring forth and manifest our deeper potentials, the richer our soul—our responsiveness to our own experience, to other people, and to life—becomes. And the more we can serve as a channel for expressing the larger life of the spirit. The evolving soul is like a jewel that is continually shedding its impurities and growing more lustrous as it becomes ever more translucent to the sun.

Although a whole range of larger human capacities is potentially available to everyone, each of us has special access to certain qualities, as well as unique aptitudes for combining and expressing them. Every soul has its own individual, jewellike character, its own "suchness." And we each have our own unique path of soulwork—how we need to develop in order to manifest this deeper potential. Two lovers with a soul connection recognize that they can help each other move forward along this path.

As young children our suchness shines forth in a simple, spontaneous way: We simply are what we are. But in identifying with a false self, we cut ourselves off from our larger being, the vast palace of powers and potentialities that is our birthright. The soul stops developing, and we experience the painful consequences of this loss: loneliness, alienation, disempowerment, meaninglessness, and the inability to love deeply. Our soul is what suffers this loss and what spurs us to set out in search of our lost birthright.

Our soul also recognizes those who can help us in this search. Yet when we recognize potential soul partners, something about them may also be disturbing. Even though we may feel instantly attracted and magnetized to them, they also stir and shake us up. We intuitively sense that this person could help us recover certain essential, forgotten parts of ourselves, but in doing so, will bring us up against our edges, where we also fear and resist that recovery.

Worthy Opponents

So we should not romanticize this kind of connection, imagining that it will bring only sweetness and light. In many ways, it is more like finding a worthy opponent. We have met our match, someone who won't let us get away with anything that is false or that diminishes our being. While a couple's heart connection provides gentle, nurturing warmth, their soul connection provides a more intense, transformative fire. It often manifests in the form of friction, especially in the early years of a relationship, as partners challenge each other, saying, in effect: "Why are you so stuck in your ways? I want you to open up and come fully alive . . . to be more present, more flexible, more real. . . ."

If two partners confront each other like this in order to prove something or get their own way, it will only result in a power struggle between their egos. To go beyond such a battle of wills, they need to understand the deeper nature of their struggle: They are actually rubbing up against the bars of each other's soul-cages. This friction, if handled consciously, can rouse them out of the prison of old identities that are constricting the flow of life within and between them.

Whenever we have cut off some part of ourselves, we suffer an inner conflict that will inevitably take the form of outer conflict with those we love. If I have shut down my tenderness, then my identity as a "tough guy" will hurt my partner, and she will struggle against that. Or if I have denied my anger, I may act in passive-aggressive ways that infuriate her. The more I am stuck in some old identity, the more unavailable I am. All the ways in which I have turned away from parts of myself call out to my partner for confrontation.

Two beings who have a soul connection want to engage in a full, free-ranging dialogue and commune with each other as deeply as possible. When I place some part of myself off limits, I am essentially saying to my partner, "I refuse to be conscious in this place. I refuse to include this in our dialogue. Stay out." This makes her feel that we don't have an unconditional connection; that I can't be fully present with her; and that she will always have to watch out for "no trespassing" signs and risk being hurt by my defensive barbed wire. If she feels strongly enough about our deeper bond, she will sometimes have to fight for it by taking on the ego-tyrant in me who is trying to control what I let in and what I let happen between us.

Sacred Combat

When we resist our partner's confrontations, because they threaten the status quo our ego strives to maintain, the soul struggle between us begins in earnest. We may try to defend ourselves by rationalizing our behavior or invalidating the other's observations. This only forces our partner to shout all the louder to be heard. And that in turn leads us to dig deeper into our battle trenches. Such conflicts are likely to escalate and destroy the relationship unless we both can see them as opportunities for soul-work.

Often we resist our partner's confrontations because they threaten to blow our cover, exposing parts of us we have a hard time acknowledging. Yet in blowing our cover, our partner is actually doing us a favor. For as long as we identify with this cover—believing we *are* the cover—we will remain alienated from who we really are.

There is a Sufi story about a lion, separated from his real parents at birth, who grows up with a flock of sheep. This lion cub acts like a sheep because he believes he is one. He lives in a sheep trance.

All of us suffer from a similar case of mistaken identity: We are a depth of soul masquerading as petty egos. We are lions believing we are sheep, hiding behind a sheep facade. As long as we think we're sheep, however, we are bound to suffer. How can a lion be happy living like a sheep? There is no way to experience true enjoyment or fulfillment when we are not being who we really are.

Someone with whom we have a soul connection sees the lion in us, hidden behind the sheep facade. Nonetheless, when our lover does us the favor of seeing through our facade, we often put up a fight. Having lost touch with our lion nature, we may have become attached to our sheep identity. Without it, we fear that we will lose our bearings, or perhaps be nothing at all. For example, a man who has lost touch with his sense of basic goodness may have settled for being a "good guy" instead. When his partner sees through this facade, he may feel panicky at first. His sheep trick doesn't work, but he still doesn't know that he is a lion either.

Such moments bring us to the razor's edge, that moment of transition when an old identity starts to break open, but nothing definite has yet emerged to take its place. If we run in fear from this experience, we will never discover the lion we really are. It is only through opening to this edge and facing our fear of nothingness that we can discover the truth: that we are something much more powerful and real than any of our self-created identities.

So when someone we love challenges our facade, if we can see this as an occasion for soulwork, rather than for victory or defeat, we create a new context for this kind of conflict. *It becomes sacred combat.*

Keith was initially attracted to Melissa because of her generosity of spirit. Everything about her——her warmth, her smile, her capacity to lavish affection, her emotional expressiveness, her ease with money——expressed this quality of abundance. Although Keith loved these qualities in her, he found himself feeling threatened by them as he experienced them lacking in himself. Where Melissa was emotionally expansive, Keith felt shut down——it was as though his arteries couldn't carry enough blood, his lungs couldn't hold enough air. In truth, his body couldn't carry and express large emotional energies because he had closed down these channels as a child, in order not to be overwhelmed by an emotionally intrusive mother.

In their typical conflict, Melissa would express discontent with some way in which Keith's austerity and constrictedness affected her, while he became defensive, acting in an angry, controlling manner. He would try to tone her down and put a lid on her energy, while she remained intent on shaking him loose. As the conflict between their different strategies escalated, their fights would grow increasingly fierce.

In examining the deeper source of their conflict, Keith eventually saw that Melissa was forcing him, by her very presence in his life, to confront the ways he remained constricted. Just by being who she was, Melissa served as an important teacher by rattling the bars of his soul-cage, inviting and urging him to expand and embody a larger quality of aliveness.

Their struggle contained an important teaching for Melissa as well. Because she had grown up in a repressive family, she had come to believe that any self-restraint or detachment was a form of death. However, her emotional extravagance often veered into self-indulgence. When she became swept up in her feelings, she would exaggerate their significance, and this often left them both feeling hurt and confused. Melissa had something important to learn from Keith in this regard—about not always acting out her feelings, or believing that something was true just because she felt strongly about it. By confronting Melissa's emotional tyrannies, Keith had a grounding effect on her; in learning to reflect on her feelings before rushing into action, she was able to settle into herself in a new way.

As Keith and Melissa came to appreciate how they were each other's teachers, this helped them see their conflict in a new light—as part of a creative and fruitful "holy war," rather than as just a divisive struggle. This is what a soul connection is about—two people joining together to nurture, stimulate, and provoke important steps in each other's unfolding.

Softening and Bravery

Life would certainly be easier if we chose a partner who only accommodated or deferred to us. Yet because our soul wants to free itself from old identities that confine us, we often pick someone instead who pushes our buttons, who rattles the bars of our soul-cage and puts us in touch with uncomfortable feelings we tried to banish long ago. If our aim is to become more conscious in a relationship, it is important to acknowledge that something in us really does want to be shaken up like this, even though our ego may resist it.

Holding a larger vision of relationship can help us rise to this challenge, by reminding us, when our partner starts rattling our cage, that this is for a larger good: to help us ripen and unfold. When we see such friction as part of our soulwork, our struggle to be more genuine and real, it takes on a sacred rather than a destructive quality. It can become an artful dance, like aikido, which involves using an opponent's attack as an opportunity to fall, or roll, above all to learn to move fluidly without rigidifying. The purpose of the struggle is to soften you— by helping you discover that you are something deeper, richer, and more fluid than any ego identity you are holding on to.

From this perspective, your partner is not an adversary, but someone who serves your development. In aikido and other Eastern martial arts, you always bow to your opponent, as a way of expressing what your soul would like to declare: "I honor and respect you as a worthy opponent, and value the opportunity to learn and grow through this combat with you." It is no accident that the metaphors of love and war—of pursuit and surrender—are often associated. The god of love, armed with arrows to penetrate our hard exterior, shatters our complacent facades, and pierces us to the core.

Approaching relationship conflict in this spirit makes it training for becoming a warrior, in the sacred, rather than the worldly, sense of that term. In his book, *Shambhala: The Sacred Path of the Warrior*, Chögyam Trungpa defines *warrior* as "one who is brave." Bravery involves a willingness to let our defenses and hiding places be exposed, so that we can open more fully to life. To be a warrior in a relationship means being willing to face our pain and fear, instead of always trying to avoid them.

Of course it will be difficult to open ourselves like this, or to soften in the conflict, unless we also share a heart connection where we feel that our partner basically loves and accepts us as we are. There has to be good faith and good will on both sides. When we have a connection based on good faith and good will, then anything our partner has to tell us about ourselves will contain some truth we can benefit from hearing. Of course our first reaction may be defensive: "I don't want to hear this." It may take a while before we can acknowledge the truth in what our partner is saying, before we can let the message in, and admit, "Well, maybe she has a point."

This is how we usually need to relax our defenses at first—by opening the door a little crack at a time, instead of forcefully trying to push the defenses aside. Above all, it is important to be kind to ourselves in moments when we feel threatened by what our partner is saying. If we blame or attack ourselves when our partner shows us some unpleasant truth about ourselves, this will only make us contract and harden all the more. Being kind to ourselves provides support when we most need it. And this inner support lends us courage, so that we can relax our defenses and hear our partner's concerns.

Thus softening and bravery go hand in hand. In Trungpa's words, "Discovering fearlessness comes from working with the softness of the human heart." Otherwise, "bravery is brittle, like a china cup. If you drop it, it will break." This combination of courage and tenderness is essential for a conscious relationship. It allows us to hear the difficult things those we love have to tell us, and to learn the soul lessons that will help us liberate the lion that we are.

Chapter Five

OVERCOMING THE ENEMY

> *Whenever we hate someone, we are hating some part of ourselves that we see in that person. We don't get worked up about anything that is not in ourselves.*
>
> HERMANN HESSE

> *Perhaps everything terrible is, in its deepest essence, something helpless that needs our love.*
>
> RAINER MARIA RILKE

In describing the marriage between Frieda and D. H. Lawrence, their friend Mabel Dodge Luhan once wrote: "What in the first days must have been the passionate attention of love...had become the attack and the defense between enemies." This is a common experience with couples. Though my partner may at one moment be my favorite person in the world, the next moment I might see her as an Attila the Hun intent on trampling me into the dust. Despite the sacred nature of our connection with those we love, we may still wind up reacting to them as though they were a threat to our very survival.

The Inner Enemy

This kind of reaction often starts to happen when a relationship brings up feelings—perhaps intense passion, fear, anger, or vulnerability—that we have never learned to tolerate. All of us have certain feelings and experiences that we find especially hard to handle. And when we grow up in a family or society that does not teach us how to accept and relate to the whole range of our experience, but instead regards many feelings as unwelcome or taboo, this creates an added difficulty: We assume there is something wrong with us when these unacceptable feelings arise. In this way, we associate certain feelings with a sense of badness or unworthiness—which is maintained by the voice of our "inner critic," who frequently scolds us for failing to measure up (to Other's standards). Since it is painful to acknowledge this "bad self," we rarely face it directly; it operates as an unconscious identity.

Becoming intimate with another person means being seen as we are, which inevitably brings to light any feeling we have tried to avoid or suppress. If we secretly believe that we are bad for having such feelings, then when this evidence of our "bad self" comes to light, we will react defensively. Yet in reacting to our partner as a threat, we externalize what is essentially an inner battle: We are treating some aspect of our experience—that we regard as bad or unacceptable—as an enemy we must defend ourselves against.

The antidote to this inner division and warfare, which keeps us on the lookout for enemies, lies in reversing the logic of self-rejection. This means opening to whatever we have closed off inside ourselves—learning to *acknowledge* and *allow* our experience, as it is, and *connect with it more directly*.

Fear, for instance, is a feeling that begins to relax and loosen up when we acknowledge it and give it space. But contracting against our fear makes it more complex and formidable, by adding to it inner division, struggle, and stress. Whenever we try to seal off painful or unpleasant feelings, they resist and bounce back at us with greater force. They appear to be an enemy that is attacking or undermining us.

Thus the very act of rejecting a feeling *makes* it Other, *makes* it threatening, *makes* it into an enemy. Never having learned that we can relate to our experience in a friendly way, we come to live in an armed camp of our own construction. And we continually act out this inner warfare in our relations with others.

Tom was a man I worked with whose relationships suffered from his deep-seated belief that vulnerable feelings were something to avoid at any cost. As a single child growing up with two overcontrolling parents, he had developed a strong aversion to feeling helpless—which he associated with being a loser.

Since Tom regarded feelings of helplessness as an enemy, he tried to guard against them by fabricating a conscious identity as someone who was always in control, a winner. He regarded this identity as "self"—who he really was. And he treated whatever threatened this image as Other and as enemy.

Feelings of helplessness, however, are part of being human. We were born helpless and we will probably die helpless. And we are bound to feel this way sometimes in relationships because we cannot really control those we love—who they are and how they affect us. Having to be on guard against such feelings requires constant vigilance, which prevents us from having open, trusting relations with people. If we want to sustain a deep, enriching relationship in our lives, we need to make friends with the whole spectrum of our experience, in all its terrors and joys.

Thus Tom needed to learn to tolerate vulnerable feelings and become more accepting of them. But this was impossible as long as he regarded them as a sign that there was something basically wrong with him.

Bad Self/Bad Other

In the mirror of intimate relationship, we all want our partner to see our intrinsic beauty and value. However, most of us don't recognize or appreciate our basic goodness ourselves. Instead, we see ourselves in terms of a false self-image, and then try to get others to affirm or admire this facade, imagining that this will make us feel good about ourselves. Yet even if we do win this approval, it doesn't truly satisfy us because it is not what we most deeply desire. What we really need is to know the intrinsic goodness of our nature, beyond anyone's conditional notions of good or bad.

Tom's efforts to prove that he was a winner were futile, since the "good self" he was trying to establish was only an image in his mind, based on trying to vanquish the equally illusory notion that he was bad for sometimes feeling helpless. How could he ever prove, once and for all, that he was a winner as long as he secretly feared he was a loser? Both identities—winner and loser, good self and bad self—were part of a trance, fantasies in his mind that prevented him from experiencing a more basic, unconditional sense of value.

As long as Susan went along with Tom's good-self facade, he was friendly and at ease. But whenever helpless feelings started to come up for him in their relationship, threatening to expose the bad-self loser, he would turn against her. On her side, Susan was at a loss to understand why he would suddenly grow cold and critical, for no apparent reason. She did not realize that at such times he was cutting himself off from his own experience, and that this inevitably cut him off from her as well. Tom's aggression toward Susan was an outer enactment of his own inner aggression—treating his more vulnerable feelings as a hated enemy.

In attacking himself when he felt helpless, Tom was doing to himself what he most feared from others. And his aggression toward himself maintained and reinforced a sense of himself as someone who was continually subject to attack. Most of us go about perpetuating a bad-self identity in a similar way. For example, we might deny our needs because we imagine they could never be met. But this only maintains an inner sense of deprivation, making our needs more exaggerated and insistent, and reinforcing an underlying view of ourselves as a needy person.

Not seeing how we create this kind of pain for ourselves, we imagine that other people are making us suffer. Thus Tom continually imagined that Other—whether his partner, his work, or the world at large—was out to control him. This mechanism of projection—looking for the source of our bad feelings outside us, focusing on what our partner does as a way to divert attention from what goes on inside us—is the most common defense strategy in relationships. And it presents a tremendous barrier to genuinely seeing, hearing, or understanding another person.

Often when a bad-self identity becomes activated inside us, we project an image of the bad Other onto our partner, and move into a position of fight or flight, attack or withdrawal. The bad Other is a generalized image of what we find most threatening in other people, based on old pain from the past. So when Tom started to feel helpless, he would see Susan as his oppressor, someone who was trying to manipulate him and make him feel bad, as his parents had.

Tom could not see what he was doing until Susan finally threatened to leave him. Then, with my help, he gradually came to see his tendency to create an enemy in his life, and how this arose from his aversion to feeling helpless. As he learned to let himself have this feeling, instead of hating himself for it, he found that it was not as horrible as he imagined.

This led to an important discovery: that helplessness was *only* a feeling. *It did not mean anything about who he was*—in particular, that he was a loser. As long as he did not create an identity out of the feeling or attach a story to it—such as "It's not manly to feel like this" or "I could be crushed"—he found that it was tolerable. In sum, Tom realized: This feeling is not who I am; it is not intrinsically bad or wrong; in fact, when I let myself experience it, the contraction around my heart melts and I become more fully present in my body, in my relationship, and in my life; and that actually makes me feel good about myself.

In this way, Tom discovered what it was like to "find his seat"—to discover a sense of composure and confidence that came from being present with his experience. He described this as feeling like a mountain, which remains unshakable even when attacked by howling storms. The more he experienced himself in this fuller way, the more his bad-self identity began to lose its hold, thereby freeing him to be more open in his relationship and his life as a whole. This gave him a whole new sense of empowerment. He was overcoming his need to create an enemy in his life.

Taking Responsibility for Our Experience

Whenever we encounter some threatening or intolerable feeling, we have a choice. We can see it as part of what we are going through and learn to relate to it, or we can react against it and look for someone to blame. When we blame

our partner—"Why are *you* making me feel this way?"—
we are, in effect, saying, "I hate my experience right now;
it's all wrong, and it's your fault." Then we might try to
make our partner different so that we don't have to feel
this way.

In the case of one couple I worked with, the woman
felt chronic dissatisfaction with her life, but instead of
owning that as her experience, she would angrily criticize
her partner for not being there for her. When I asked her
what she would feel if he were more available, she said,
"Joy." Her partner in turn blamed her for being so critical.
When I asked him what he would feel if she were more
accepting, he said, "Peace and self-assurance." In effect, the
woman was saying, "I can only feel joy if *he* is more present," while the man was saying, "I can only feel at peace
with myself if *she* accepts me." As a result, they remained
stuck in a vicious circle: she attacking when he withdrew,
seeing him as the cause of her unhappiness; he withdrawing when she attacked, seeing her as the cause of his
distress.

Nothing could change until they were each willing to
take responsibility for their own experience: she for her
chronic dissatisfaction, he for his insecurity. When she
became willing to look within herself for the source of joy,
she no longer needed to attack him for depriving her of
happiness; and when he became willing to look within
himself for the source of peace and self-assurance, he no
longer had to distance himself because she failed to provide that for him.

To regard our partner as the source of our happiness or
misery is to abdicate responsibility for our own experience.
Responsible means "able to respond." Becoming responsible
for our experience means *being able to respond to it,* as it is.
Responding to our experience starts with caring about what
we are going through and inquiring into it, instead of
judging it or pushing it away. In responding to our experi-

ence in this way, we also cultivate loving-kindness toward ourselves and greater self-awareness.

Cultivating Awareness and Loving-Kindness

Loving-kindness is a term often used in the Buddhist tradition to indicate a state of unconditional friendliness, benevolence, and goodwill. It is akin to the Christian term *charity*, a word that comes from the Latin *caritas*, the root of our word *caring*. Substituting *loving-kindness* for *charity* in the King James version of St. Paul's famous letter to the Corinthians helps us see how crucial this quality is:

> Though I speak with the tongues of men and of angels, and have not loving-kindness, I am become as sounding brass, or a tinkling cymbal.
>
> And though I have the gift of prophecy, and understand all mysteries, and all knowledge; and though I have all faith, so that I could remove mountains, and have not loving-kindness, I am nothing.
>
> Loving-kindness suffereth long ... envieth not ... thinketh no evil ... but rejoiceth in the truth.
>
> Loving-kindness never faileth; but where there be prophecies, they shall fail; where there be tongues, they shall cease; where there be knowledge, it shall vanish away.
>
> For we know in part, and we prophecy in part.
>
> But when that which is perfect is come, then that which is in part shall be done away.

Loving-kindness contains an inner perfection, as Paul suggests, because it is an expression of our true nature. Without it, no real happiness is possible.

Loving-kindness starts at home by caring for ourselves when we are having a hard time. Once we can extend this kind of compassion toward ourselves, we can more readily feel this way toward others. This counteracts our tendency to regard Other as a potential enemy.

So if we are to overcome the need for an enemy—both within and without—we need to start by developing unconditional friendliness toward our own experience. Ever since childhood, most of us have tried to live up to external standards for how we should be. In learning to see ourselves as we imagine Other sees us, at the expense of our own immediate sense of who we are, we have lost touch with the capacity to rest in our own nature and trust that we could simply be ourselves, as we are. The antidote to this alienation from ourselves is to cultivate unconditional self-acceptance.

Accepting ourselves unconditionally doesn't mean mindlessly indulging in emotions or inappropriate behavior. Nor does it mean having to shower ourselves with affirmations or like everything about ourselves. In fact, liking ourselves for some *reason*—because we approve of our behavior or measure up to some standard—is *conditional* self-acceptance. Unconditional self-acceptance is of a totally different order than this; it means *letting ourselves have our experience, whatever it may be.*

Loving-kindness and deeper awareness are the elements most essential for unconditional self-acceptance, as well as for any real growth or healing. How can we cultivate these qualities? Through a willingness to *inquire into, acknowledge, allow,* and *fully open to* our experience.

First, we need to be willing to *inquire* into what is going on inside us, instead of just assuming that we know what our experience signifies and reacting automatically. Often we *think* we know what we're experiencing—"I'm angry, that's all" or "This is just an old hang-up from childhood"—without understanding what is really happening. If we reflect more deeply, we discover that there's more to any experience than we can know at first glance.

So we need to be willing to ask ourselves, "What's going on here?" and really look with an open mind, instead of assuming that we already know.

Second, we can *acknowledge* what is happening: "Yes, this is what I'm experiencing right now. I'm feeling threatened ... hurt ... angry ... defensive." Acknowledging involves recognizing and naming what is going on, as well as inviting it into awareness. We should never underestimate the power of bare acknowledgment. Simply recognizing what is happening, instead of automatically reacting to it, allows us to shift from a passive to an active stance, which already gives us greater freedom.

Third, we can learn to *allow* our experience to be there, as it is. Allowing ourselves to have our experience does not mean wallowing in feelings or acting them out. Instead, it involves giving ourselves space to have our experience—gently holding our feelings in awareness and softening around them, rather than hardening against them or imposing judgments on them. Often we have a hard time with this because we subconsciously identify with our feelings ("this anger is me") or else reject them ("this anger is not me"). So it may require some time and concentration to relate to our experience in this way.

If a feeling is particularly intense, it often helps to breathe deeply and give it plenty of space, letting it expand as far as it wants to. This releases any sense of inner pressure, which results from resisting the feeling or contracting against it. If we feel too threatened by our experience to give it space, this usually indicates that some *story*—a background judgment or belief—has become activated in our mind. Stories that interfere the most often take the form of: "If I feel this, something bad will happen," or "This feeling means something bad about me ... or about my life ... or about the other person." Acknowledging and naming these stories helps us put them aside and bring our attention back to our bodily-felt experience.

Fourth, we can let ourselves open more fully to what we are experiencing—which brings us more fully present. Instead of trying to judge, explain, or manipulate how we feel, we can simply maintain an *open presence* in the face of it. What is most important here is not *what* we are feeling, but the process of *opening* to it.

Feelings in themselves don't necessarily lead to greater wisdom, but the process of opening to them can. When our focus shifts from the feeling itself—as an object of pleasure or pain—to our state of presence with it, we move from the realm of personality into the larger space of being. Only in this larger presence can we find the resources we need to deal with our situation. And when we are present with a feeling, instead of reacting to it as good or bad, the inner war—between self and Other, between "me" and "my experience"—starts to wind down. Then our awareness can operate more unobstructedly, allowing us to perceive more clearly what is actually going on and what needs to be done.

It is often striking how something as simple as letting ourselves have our experience can immediately affect how we relate to the situation at hand. For example, when my stepson first came home from college for the summer, I found myself tense and somewhat shut down. I had been enjoying having my wife all to myself and felt reluctant to give that up. At first I judged myself for being selfish, but this only made me more tense. Clearly there was something more going on that needed my attention.

When I looked more closely at my reaction, I discovered some fear, which closing down had been a way of avoiding. As I acknowledged and allowed this fear, this helped me see that an old, exaggerated story from my past was distorting my perception: I was afraid that my needs would not be met, that I would be shunted aside. As long as I tried to stuff away my fear, I remained in a state of tension, because I was actually shunting aside my own experience. But as soon as I gave up struggling with the fear and could see it for what it was, I started to relax, and regained my seat.

Making friends with ourselves involves all these elements—inquiring, acknowledging, allowing, understanding, opening, and then, as a result, finding our seat and becoming more fully present, at one with ourselves. This kind of unconditional friendliness, born of the union of awareness and loving-kindness, is what we most wanted from our parents; it is what we seek from teachers, therapists, friends, and lovers; and ultimately it is what we need from ourselves. When we start to relate to our experience in this way, we usually find that our partner feels more responsive and connected with us as well.

Beyond the Enemy

Overcoming the need for an enemy provides access to a deeper source of energy and power in our lives. The Tibetans have a word for this larger energy—*drala*—which literally means "beyond the enemy." Chögyam Trungpa describes drala as "the magical quality of existence" that arises out of "connecting the wisdom of your own being with the power of things as they are." We can perceive the power inherent in things as they are—the radiance of fire, the solidity of earth, the expansiveness of joy, the tenderness of sorrow—only when we drop our struggle with ourselves and our experience.

Whenever I focus on what my partner is "doing to me," I lose touch with love's drala, love's magic. My energy goes into drawing battle lines and defending myself against the bad Other. But when I take responsibility for my experience, I become more present because I am connecting with myself—which can only bring us closer. This provides a general guideline for relationships: When we focus on another as the cause of our difficulties, or the solution to them, we contract and tense up; but when we acknowledge the cause or solution inside us, and relate to *that*, we start to open, expand, and settle down.

Intimate relationships and our world as a whole have so little peace because we continually externalize the battle between self and Other that rages within us. Just as the mentality that builds missile systems and spends billions on armaments has impoverished our world, so it impoverishes our soul when most of our energy in a relationship goes into defense.

Conscious relationship is a path of peacemaking and inner reconciliation. To live at peace with another human being, we need to stop rejecting our experience and make peace with whatever we have made Other inside ourselves.

Becoming Responsible for Our Own Experience

When we experience something threatening or uncomfortable in a relationship, we tend to focus on our partner as the source of our discomfort. Yet though our partner may push our buttons, these are *our* buttons nevertheless. It is extremely important to recognize this in order to develop greater self-understanding as well as communicate more effectively with our partner.

One way to start becoming more responsible for our experience is by looking at our reactions and complaints as a mirror, which can reveal and help us relate to what is going on inside us. To do this, consider something that consistently bothers you about your partner—some way your partner treats you or something you typically blame your partner for. (If you're not in a relationship right now, think about a previous partner.) How do you see or interpret what your partner is doing? And what about this bothers you so much? Use it as a mirror. Ask yourself, "Is there a part of me like that?" or "Is there a way in which I act like that or treat myself that way?" What is it like to acknowledge this in yourself? How do you usually relate to this part of yourself? And how does it want to be related to instead?

JANET

What bothers me most is my husband's selfishness. He often seems so impersonal, so objective and detached that I don't know if he really cares about me. And nothing I do seems to make him change.

Let me ask you this, but don't answer too quickly: Is there any way that *you* are detached or selfish?

When I asked myself, "What part of me is selfish?" I felt a quick wave of nausea.

What's making you feel that way?

Well, I've always put that on men, like, "That's their problem."

So what's it like to recognize this in yourself?

It's intense.

What's intense about it?

Well, I realize that there is a way I don't give myself entirely. On the surface I give a lot, but maybe not so much on a deeper level. I can feel something that's hiding and doesn't want to give itself.

You don't have to force it to give. That's like trying to make your husband give you more. If there's a way you don't want to give yourself to another person, you probably have some good reasons for that. Inquiring into that—seeing what's going on there, being friendly toward it—will open up a path, a way forward.

Would you be willing to sit with this part of yourself and see how it feels, just as you might with a child who was feeling shy and wanted to hide? Once you connect with it in a friendly way, you might ask it, "What's the matter? Why is it so hard to give?"

What I get is that this part of me is insecure. It needs attention and caring. It needs to know that it won't be abandoned.

It needs attention and caring. Are you giving it that attention right now as we talk?

Yes.

How does that feel?

It feels good.

As you give that to yourself, notice how you feel about your husband's selfishness.

Somehow it's not such a big issue.

You feel less pressure to make him change?

Yes. I have noticed this before: When I give myself this kind of attention, I find that I have what I want in my partner.

Exactly. That's the point.

It's a law, right?

That's often how it works.

When I am giving to myself, it also opens me up to being able to receive what he has to offer.

You're more open.

So the more I give myself the attention that I deserve and have lacked, the more the relationship changes, and I get more of what I want from my partner. That's odd and strange and very beautiful.

Yes. When we are cut off from something inside ourselves, then it feels all the more urgent to get it from our partner. This urgency often has a life-or-death emotional charge. And when we direct that at others, it pushes them away.

But when you give yourself what you need, your partner feels less pressured, and that lets him move toward you. Mirroring also happens from the inside out: The more available you are for yourself, the more your partner is likely to become available. Other people tend to treat us the same way we treat ourselves.

DAN

What bothers me is my partner's tendency to deny and rationalize what is really going on. She often won't tell me the real reason why she does something.

She's not forthright and straightforward in telling you her motives. What bothers you most about that?

It doesn't feel respectful to me. If she really trusted and respected me, she wouldn't need to cover up her motives. For me, respect is the cement that holds a relationship together.

So you feel that she doesn't respect you. Is there a place inside you where you don't feel respect?

Like self-respect?

Yes. In other words, why is respect such a big issue for you? Each of us has some button that our partner pushes. Lack of respect seems to be one of your buttons.

You say that your partner doesn't tell you what's really going on, and that feels disrespectful to you. But someone else might frame that differently. He might say, "Maybe she has a hard time getting in touch with herself or knowing what's true for her." But your frame is that she doesn't respect you. That's a clue that something is going on for you in that area. What might that be?

I want to be respected.

Why is that such a big issue for you?

I grew up in a family with a brother who was eleven years older. So I always felt much younger than everyone else. I didn't feel protected, and I never developed real confidence in myself. I guess I'm still looking at the world and saying, "Hey, respect me."

Right. Thank you for revealing that; it takes courage. This image of yourself as not worthy of respect is a conditioned belief, a soul-cage that confines you. Instead of trying so hard to get your partner to respect you, you could see that your path in this life involves freeing yourself from this particular soul-cage. As long as you're in that cage, you're going to interpret everything in your relationship in terms of respect. My guess is that when you see everything that way, your wife doesn't feel that you really see her for who she is. And if she feels that you are always judging her in your own terms, that probably makes it hard for her to be forthcoming.

When I ask her questions to get at what is really going on, she says, "I'm feeling badgered by you." I guess that's because she feels me laying my trip on her.

Right. What is it like right now to acknowledge and experience this place in you that needs respect?

It feels good to recognize this. A little shaky, but good.

That's because you are going inward and connecting with yourself, instead of looking outside yourself for the solution. In using this difficulty as a mirror, you start to see what needs to be addressed or healed within yourself. And that allows a new direction or path to open up.

CHRISTINE

I keep feeling that I want more passion and strength from my partner, Peter. I want him to be more decisive and committed, to feel his anger directly, and to set his boundaries with me. I want him to meet me in a challenging way. I feel like a hungry wolf—I really need to know: "Are you here with me right now?"

You want him to be more passionately engaged with you, is that it?

Yes.

Is there a way in which you're not passionate and engaged with yourself?

No (laughs) . . . *Well, maybe.*

Do you want to say something about that?

I'm most aware of that when I feel strongly about something.

Instead of allowing myself to have my strong convictions, I tend to think, "Wait a second, I shouldn't really be saying this. It's not my place." I don't feel that I have a right to say, "This is what I believe," and be really direct. I water down my spontaneous responses.

Isn't that the sort of thing you can't stand seeing Peter do?

Yes. Every time he shies away from confrontation, or takes forever to answer a question, or doesn't look me in the eye, or fidgets with his hands while I'm talking to him——when I see that kind of avoidance, I just go crazy.

So you recognize that you also undercut yourself that way.

Yes.

What's it like to acknowledge that this is *your* issue?

(Long pause) I have a feeling of sadness and loss. . . . It's a feeling of being incomplete, a sense of betrayal somewhere deep inside. . . . It feels like a quiet sense of separation from my soul.

I could feel you in touch with something very juicy and alive just then. It was quite tangible. Right there——in that moment of acknowledging your separation from your soul——you are starting to find a path. In being responsible for your own experience, you actually start to reconnect with your soul——which is what you most want——instead of trying to get that from your partner——which only frustrates you.

Right, it's an uphill battle.

But when you touched that raw place in yourself, you softened. Could you feel that?

Yes. It's a strange thing, though. I do contact this place when I'm alone, and I feel in touch with myself when I do. But it's so delicate. It doesn't take much for me to lose the presence of those tender, soulful places in me or those powerful places that I struggle to value. And when I'm with Peter and he is not putting himself forward strongly, then I feel unsupported in this effort.

Have you ever shown him how you struggle to find this deep sense of connection with yourself?

Yes. . . . Well I think so, but I'm not sure.

Would you be willing to do that right now? Let him in on what it's like for you.

(To Peter) Every second of my life, there's a possibility that I could leave my soul behind. This feels like a life-or-death issue to me. I value staying in touch with myself more than anything, but some part of me doesn't seem to value it at all. I struggle with this all the time. And when I'm not struggling with it, I tend to just go to sleep. And it's really hard for me to acknowledge this part of myself that just wants to go to sleep.

How does it feel to share that with him?

I feel very open and very seen.

(To Peter) I feel like you're really getting a glimpse of me. And it's great to have you just sitting there right now. I feel that you're really here with me.

Do you know why he's so present with you? Most people would find it easy to be there that way with you right now—because *you're* so there with you.

What's true is that you really have to work at staying connected to your soul. But in your relationship you usually take the position of the one who's connected and passionate, who says, "Let's connect, let's grow, let's be more alive." You see yourself as the passionate one, while you identify Peter as "out of it." He mirrors back to you your own tendency to disconnect, which you usually deny in yourself and fight against when you see it in him.

PETER: *It feels so much better to me when she can acknowledge this. What usually happens is that I feel accused of being separate from my soul. And that keeps us from really meeting.*

(To Peter) So you feel more connected to her when she acknowledges this. And you don't feel blamed or pushed away.

PETER: *Yes. It's a relief because now we're both in the same place, dealing with the same issue, together, instead of her being the expert and me being the oaf.*

(To Christine) When you become responsible for your own experience, and you let Peter in on your struggle, things open up between you, and you move closer. Then he can be on your side in that struggle, and it becomes something you're both working on: "This is *our* issue—we *both* have a hard time staying present and being real."

That's what I want. But when I am separated from myself, it's incredibly painful to feel the part of me that doesn't want to be present, that wants to leave. It's hard to own that as part of me, or to let Peter or anyone see that. I feel a profound sense of shame about it.

When you were revealing it just now, did you feel shame then?

Not so much. I felt it a little, but it wasn't taking up all the space.

I felt your courage coming through more than any sense of shame.

When we turn away from something in ourselves, we often project it onto others and see them as an enemy in this regard, which shuts down the flow of energy in a relationship. On the other hand, when we relate to what is going on in ourselves, this opens up the energy. The trick is to use our criticism of the other as a mirror to help us see what we are cut off from in ourselves.

With Christine, I simply asked her, "Is there a part of you that's like what you reject in Peter?" Then she looked inside and said, "Yes, there *is* a way I turn away from my own soul." At the moment she acknowledged that, she also started to reclaim her soul. That was a moment of *drala*, ordinary magic. It was impossible not to feel connected with her at that moment.

Peter may also have a hard time staying connected with himself, but when Christine projects *her* disconnection onto him as well, he has to struggle under a double load. And that makes it much harder for him to connect with her. But as soon as she acknowledged how she wasn't fully present herself, Peter felt relieved of the burden of her projection. He immediately became more present and engaged with her, which is what she really wants.

This does not negate the fact that there may also be valid ways in which we want our partner to act differently. That's fine, as long as trying to change our partner is not a substitute for work we need to do on ourselves.

ROGER

Most of my worst fights with my wife start out as arguments about time. I'm a schedule person. I like to be on time or early, but this is not a high priority for her. When we go on vacation, I start to feel uptight a week in advance, anticipating all the things she will need to do at the last minute—long after I think we should already be on our way. We've left for parties late and become so involved in fighting over this that we had to turn around and go home. Even talking about this makes me tense.

I don't see the part of me that is like what she is doing, though. I can't imagine being laid-back about time and letting someone else worry about it.

How do you see or interpret what your wife is doing?

The story in my mind is that she doesn't care about what I have to get done.

It seems to you that she's not considering you, not considering your needs?

That's right.

So is there a way that *you* are not considering your needs?

Perhaps I don't consider the need to relax . . . or not be driven by a schedule.

Yes. What's it like to acknowledge that need?

It's hard to acknowledge it because I see it as irresponsible.

That's your *judgment* about it. Of course you have a hard time recognizing your need to relax if you judge it as irresponsible. And when your wife is not adhering to your schedule, you put that same judgment on her.

Well, I know that I need to relax. The problem is in letting it happen.

How does it feel to acknowledge that need to relax?

It feels good.

What does "good" feel like?

It feels calmer and steadier.

So you start to feel more calm and relaxed just by acknowledging that need.

When you're in a time crunch, you feel tense because you aren't considering your own feelings or needs. But you're usually not aware of how you are creating your own tension. Instead, you focus on how your wife is inconsiderate. And that makes you even more uptight. So you get a double whammy—it feels as though there is no consideration for you on the inside or the outside. No wonder even talking about this makes you tense.

Being responsible for your own experience does not mean that your wife wins the power struggle, or that you have to give up your concern with being on time. But this whole issue will create less stress once you start to consider your own need to relax. Then if you still need to confront your wife about her tendency to be late, she will probably be able to hear you better, because you won't be putting all your own inner tension on her.

Yes, I can see that. Thank you.

BARBARA

Every time my husband and I have a discussion, he approaches it in a totally logical way, and I get frustrated. I'm not sure why this bothers me so much, but it feels intolerable sometimes.

I'm not clear how this situation is a mirror because I don't see an overlogical part of myself.

When he's being logical, what do you think he's doing to you or not doing for you in that moment?

He's not recognizing me.

What's not being recognized?

That I have a different way of approaching a problem and can come to an equally valid solution.

You think he's not recognizing your intelligence. Is there a part of you that doesn't recognize that in yourself?

Oh, yes, a very large part.

So you don't honor your own intelligence, but when your husband approaches things in a highly logical way, you focus on how *he* is not honoring your intelligence.

Then you get a double whammy: You feel squeezed—like Roger in his time crunch—both within and without. No wonder it feels intolerable.

Right, I can see that.

What's it like to recognize that you don't honor your intelligence, and that you need that kind of honoring?

It brings me to an edge. It's scary.

Can you allow that fear to be here? Give it plenty of room.

I always wanted my parents to recognize that I was a bright child, and to say, "Wow, what a neat person you are!" I was the oldest of four, and took care of my siblings, but no one ever looked after me.

You want to feel recognized and valued. Can you let yourself acknowledge that desire?

That feels better—like I'm moving through space now, instead of stuck. It feels softer.

Are you able to recognize your intelligence right now?

Yes. I feel grounded in myself.

From here, how does your husband's logical mind look to you?

It doesn't seem so threatening. It's just his logical mind, and that's all right. It's just the way he is.

Right. It's not so threatening, because you are recognizing yourself. How could his intelligence threaten you, if you recognize and value your own intelligence? How could it?

No, it can't. It can't.

His intelligence only threatens you when you don't honor your own. That's how it is in all the situations we're looking at here. Our partner's lack of acknowledgment is especially threatening when it mirrors some way we don't acknowledge ourselves. How our partner treats us becomes particularly intolerable when it reminds us of some painful way we treat ourselves.

Most of the time we are much more aware of how our partner treats us than we are of how we treat ourselves. The mirroring exercise turns this around, letting us see how our own mind creates what we react to "out there."

Another person might experience your husband's logical mind as helpful, but for you it is demeaning. How you react to what he does is a reflection of your own sore points. Otherwise, you would just see it as his stuff: "Okay, there he is being overlogical again. I have compassion for him and hope he'll learn that this isn't the only way to be." It wouldn't upset you so much *because it wouldn't mean anything about you.*

If we regard relationship as a mirror, then whatever upsets us can provide useful information. It becomes a red flag pointing to something that needs to be related to, healed, contacted, or loved inside us. Then when our partner pushes our buttons, instead of saying, "What's the matter with you?" we could say, "Some button of mine is being pushed. Let me see what that is." That's what's called "becoming responsible for our own experience."

LAWRENCE

I am highly sensitive to my partner's disapproval of me. When she says something critical, I feel angry with her and bad about myself. It seems that she does this a lot, and I don't know what to do about it.

And what does this reflect in you?

I seem to be addicted to putting myself down. I've tried to be compassionate toward myself for behavior that I don't like, but it doesn't seem to work. It's as though I need to punish myself.

There's a way that you think you're not good enough?

Yes.

What's it like to acknowledge that you take this to be the truth about yourself—that you're not good enough?

It strikes me as very sad.

Can you let yourself feel that sadness?

Yes. It makes me want to be affectionate and respectful toward myself.

Do you want that?

Oh, indeed I do. But the fact that I haven't gotten there worries me.

When you say, "I want to love and respect myself," can you feel that right now?

It's a good feeling. It's something I do want.

Can you actually let yourself *feel that wanting* right now? What's that like?

Well, I tell you, it's strong. The very fact that I'm tuning into that wavelength, rather than the negative one, makes me feel strong. It feels very positive.

Yes. Since that desire—to recognize your basic goodness—comes from your soul, to feel that wanting is to be in touch with your soul.

That feels good, just thinking that.

Don't just *think* it, though.

Right, feel it.

Let yourself feel that wanting *in your body*. It's important to emphasize that a bit. The desire has its own energy.

That wanting is a real force. I'm a poet, and this makes me want to write a poem about it. I haven't thought of "wanting" except in a negative way—that I have no right to "want" somehow.

To feel our desire is one of the most powerful forces there is, especially when what we're wanting is our own being or some aspect of our being. We could call this a *holy longing*. It's not just a trivial thing.

No, not at all.

It's important for you to let yourself feel the energy in your longing. Can you let yourself dive into this longing?

Yes, I can. It's a very different feeling in my system. I'm not used to it.

Yes. Instead of struggling with the critic—"I shouldn't judge myself so much," or, "I wish I liked myself more"—you can simply acknowledge what is—that you really want to know your own value. Recognizing and honoring that desire is the antidote to the critic.

I can feel that.

What does it feel like?

I'm already more in touch with myself, more here with myself, less self-critical.

Yes. Recognizing the holy longing already puts you in touch with what you desire. As the Indian poet Kabir wrote, "It is the intensity of the longing that does all the work."

From this place, if your partner were criticizing you and you needed to say no to that, could you do so?

Yes.

How does that feel?

Great. There's tremendous power in that.

Yes. So if your partner continually criticizes you, the question is why you let that happen, why you have not made it clear that this is not okay with you. You let that happen because her critic resonates and collaborates with your critic. When you acknowledged your own self-criticism, that brought up sadness. And out of that sadness there arose a powerful longing. . . .

I want to let the longing have that power. . . . It has the power, but to acknowledge it. . . .

Yes, to acknowledge it, and feel it. This holy longing is like a flame. When we're longing for our true self, then all our false identifications burn up in that fire. Instead of struggling with the false identification—"I'm not good enough. How do I change that?"—the secret is to stoke the fire that can burn it up.

You're writing the poem.

Well, in this place we are all poets.

SHARON

I have a hard time when my husband doesn't let me know he loves me on a regular basis. I start to push and badger him to tell me he loves me, but I think he's afraid of expressing love openly. When I looked in the mirror, I became aware that the connectedness I want with him I'm not giving myself.

So there's a way in which you don't feel that loving or connected with yourself.

Yes. It's a place where I am really hard on myself for having problems and for not getting through them fast enough.

This part of you that doesn't move as fast as you think it should: How does it want to be related to? What does it need?

It needs rest.

Rest from what?

I need rest from demands.

Rest from demands, that's right. See if you can give yourself that rest right now. What is it like to let yourself have your experience right now, with no demand that it be any other way, or that you be any other way?

I feel stuck right here. I feel like I'm not good enough. (crying.)

And how does that affect you?

It's like a block in my heart.

See if you can just feel that block, acknowledge it, allow it, breathe into it, and let the tears happen.

It feels scary and vulnerable. It puts me in touch with a place where I feel unloved. . . . Revealing this is not something I would normally do. Usually I can't even get close to it, but now I am.

Good. See what it feels like to let that fear come up and be here.

All I can see is this little girl who hid under a table and didn't want to come out because she was so scared. That was how I felt as a child—really alone and scared, not knowing that my feelings were of any value. I feel a shaking in my body that always happened as a child when I would get close to my feelings.

That's the child's fear. She doesn't know that she can have her feelings and that they're okay, because there was never any support for that. It's important to recognize this as how the child felt.

Right now, when you say that . . . You know, I've told my story to a lot of people, but I didn't want to really feel it because it's scary to make all that real. I feared that if I made it real, I'd be crazy. Thinking about that makes me want to go numb and close down.

You started that by saying, "right now ..." Come back to "right now." You don't have to get stuck in that old story. Right now you're so present with what is happening that you are acknowledging both your fear and your tendency to go numb. Those vulnerable, shaky feelings are there, but there's also someone who's willing to face them.

What do you mean, "There's someone ... ?"

In other words, some part of you is also willing to look at what's happening. Alongside the scared child, there's another part of you that's showing up right now— your inner warrior. Being a warrior does not mean always feeling strong and all-together, but being willing to go where we feel most shaky and un-together. That is who is showing up right now, alongside the scared child.

I think she's someone I lost a long time ago.

Is she lost right now?

I'm not sure.

Well, how are you feeling?

Right now I feel real about what I am experiencing. And I haven't been doing that—being real with what I feel.

What is it like now, right now, to feel real like this?

My ears are burning. I feel more sensitive ... it's like a kindness, a sweetness.

So when you gave yourself a rest from demands, you felt fear at first; but now as you let yourself have your experience, you feel more real, and there's some kindness, some sweetness. It's important to notice these experiential changes that occur as we start to pay attention inwardly.

Yes. There's a lightness now, and I can feel some joy coming in. I also feel myself more now.

You *feel yourself* more—there it is, the antidote. That's the antidote to everything, really—experiencing that direct connection with yourself. The antidote is in the poison. In other words, the way to connect with yourself is to start where you are, which in this case meant acknowledging your fear and lack of self-love. And when you opened to that, you began to feel more real, more in touch.

This reminds me of Rilke's words: "Perhaps all the dragons in our lives are only princesses who are only waiting to see us act just once with beauty and courage"—by facing and acknowledging what we are going through. That kind of kindness and presence is the medicine for all our old poisons. And it's what allows the beauty in you to come out, as is happening right now.

It's good to be here, in a place where I feel safe to experience my pain and can find compassion for it.

What creates that safety here is that we're creating a space where we can be present with our experience as it is. That's what we needed as a child too. Yet because we didn't learn how to *let be*, we developed all these defensive strategies in order to *make do*.

This is also one of the greatest gifts we can offer those we love—this space in which they can acknowledge and touch what they're experiencing. This is one of the greatest expressions of loving-kindness.

So instead of badgering your husband to tell you he loves you, you might share with him what goes on for you, and also encourage him, give him space to tell you what goes on for him when you ask him to express his love. That might help him contact and free up something he is having a hard time with too—maybe he doesn't acknowledge himself either. Then this problem that seems so difficult could provide an opportunity to connect with each other in a much deeper way.

Chapter Six

COEMERGENT REALITIES

The elixir is hidden in the poison.

RUMI

Deep relationships always contain enormous transformative potential because they bring out the best *and* the worst in us. While love makes us want to melt the rigid defenses that keep us from living more expansively, this desire to melt also threatens the conditioned personality, which hardens its defenses to preserve the status quo. Though we may truly desire to connect with another soul-to-soul, our ego still prefers to promote and defend self-image instead. That is why we often feel pulled in opposite directions when we are in love. We become acutely aware of straddling a breach between two different sides of ourselves—unconditional love and conditioned fears, our small self and our larger being—that seem to work at cross-purposes inside us. Yet here at this juncture, where we feel the sharp contrast between our desire to expand and our desire to contract, is where real transformation becomes possible.

One Ground, Two Paths

Western philosophy and religion have often explained the tension between our larger being and our tendency to turn away from it as the result of two irreconcilable cosmic forces—good vs. evil, godly vs. satanic, spirit vs. flesh—at war inside us. Yet this dualistic perspective turns the polar tension at the core of our nature into a crippling opposition. If we are to work creatively with the challenging edge love brings us to, we need a new way of understanding and handling our inner contradictions.

Instead of regarding love and fear, expansion and contraction, yes and no, as symptoms of warring forces within us, we could also see them as both arising from the same source: the basic openness of our nature. Sometimes we recognize and trust this openness as a reservoir of love, creativity, and good will. When this happens, we want to reach out and take risks. ("I feel so open, I could embrace the whole world.") At other times we do not trust this openness. Instead, we see it as a threat to our survival, thereby turning it into a cause for fear, a reason to contract and defend. ("I feel so open, I could be crushed.") Nonetheless, these two different impulses—to expand in love or contract in fear, to melt or to harden—both arise as responses to a single truth: Our nature is essentially wide open, rather than a closed box with sealed-off boundaries.

Thus we have a choice at every moment—to turn toward our true nature or away from it, to live in accord with soul's desire to awaken or with ego's tendency to remain entrenched behind its defenses. This situation is described in the Buddhist tradition as "one ground, two paths."

Coemergence

Yet moving forward in our lives is rarely as easy as choosing one path and rejecting the other, because we usually have one foot in each world: We are partly closed and partly open, partly fearful and partly brave, partly confused and partly clear. While the intrinsic nature of our awareness is open and transparent, like water, much of the time it remains clouded by conditioned beliefs, which function like dirt suspended in the water. Borrowing a term from Tibetan Buddhism, we could say that our natural clarity and conditioned tendencies are *coemergent:* They arise together, or coemerge, side by side. Our experience is a mix of clarity and confusion, conscious aims and unconscious influences. We are usually half awake and half asleep.

So even though we may want to be more fully alive and present, we remain influenced by unconscious factors—old attachments, identities, fears, and projections— that distort our experience and diminish our capacities. Nonetheless, no matter how lost or shut down we are, the sun of awareness is always shining brightly behind the clouds of our confused beliefs. Even in our darkest moments the light of clarity and wakefulness is near at hand. As soon as I recognize where I am—"I am confused, I am lost"—I start to wake up from my confusion and find myself again. *My awareness* of being lost, confused, or stuck *is never itself lost, confused, or stuck.* In recognizing how out of touch I am, I am already more in touch. And in admitting to my partner, "I know that I hurt you," the awareness that recognizes this is not itself hurtful. Whenever we act in a petty or unconscious way, we can always self-correct by becoming aware of, and acknowledging, what we're doing.

To use a different analogy: Our awareness is like a movie screen on which our ego dramas play themselves out. Though we usually don't notice this larger, open backdrop, because we are so absorbed in the movie, the screen is what enables us to see the movie in the first place. Moreover, this screen is never corrupted or damaged by what happens in the film. If there is a fire in the movie, the screen does not burn up; if there is a murder, it does not get bloody. No matter how caught up we are in our dramas, when we tap into our awareness, it is always larger than *any* drama, *any* emotion, *any* state of mind. As a great Indian Tantric yogi, Tilopa, once said, "The nature of mind is like space; therefore there is nothing that it cannot encompass." This encompassing quality of our larger awareness is what people often discover and come to know more deeply through meditation. It is always available as a resource to help us awaken from our trance and become more present. All we have to do is turn our attention toward it.

The antidote to any poison in our psyche always lies close at hand. Indeed, every poison calls for a specific antidote, which can only be discovered through turning toward awareness, through acknowledging where we are and what is going on with us, no matter how unpleasant it seems to be. If we are devoured by jealousy, for example, we need to see what is happening here: We are caught in a trance, in which we feel insecure because we imagine that we're not as good as someone else, that Other is more beautiful, valuable, or lovable than self. As we see our insecurity and the pain it causes, the antidote also becomes available: We find a new desire coming alive in us—to free ourselves from our negative self-image, to know and trust in our value. Thus our jealousy points in the direction of confidence, which is the only real antidote for jealousy. In this way, every state of mind, when held in the space of our larger awareness, will reveal its own remedy.

Uncovering the Genuine Impulse

The truth of coemergence—that everything has two sides, that clarity and confusion are usually intertwined in our experience—has another important implication for relationships as well. It means that even the most confused or distorted behavior contains some genuine impulse hidden within it.

For example, if we continually struggle to win approval from others, this behavior may be misguided, but it also points to a deeper desire underneath: We want to affirm our basic goodness. Similarly, our defensive attempts to make ourselves hard and impenetrable, to establish ourselves as someone to be reckoned with, may be a way of trying to feel our strength or substance. Always having to maintain control over situations is a distorted form of exercising our will. And maintaining emotional distance from others is often a misguided attempt to establish or preserve our individual integrity. Contained in these confused behaviors we find a real longing to contact some essential resource or capacity we have lost touch with: value, strength, will, or integrity.

The bad news about coemergence is that the false personality can co-opt and distort anything genuine in us. But the good news is that a certain intelligence permeates even our most distorted behavior. Therefore, instead of condemning ourselves for our pretenses and defenses, we can look for the genuine longing hidden within them. If we can bring a friendly spirit of inquiry to our confused emotions and behaviors, they can point us toward some authentic quality of our true nature, of which they are but facsimiles.

Rediscovering the Holy Longing

Mark was a middle-aged man who felt trapped by his increasingly humdrum existence. He found himself flying into unreasonable rages with his wife and indulging in fantasies of affairs with other women. Although he liked to blame his fifteen-year marriage for his paralysis, his relationship with his wife was not the real problem.

In the light of coemergence, we can understand Mark's rages and restlessness as not just neurotic, but as symptoms of an authentic urge boiling up from within him; in this case, to awaken into a richer, more vibrant connection with life. At its root this is a *holy longing* because its aim is the recovery of being; its message is "I want to be who I really am." But since Mark was not used to paying attention to the longings of his soul, he could only interpret his escape fantasies as meaning that he should leave his marriage. This was his confusion and distortion—imagining that he had to leave his wife in order to find himself.

Before Mark could discover the deeper aspiration underneath his erratic behavior, he had to start becoming responsible for his experience—by recognizing his restless feelings as a sign of something within himself calling out for attention. Acknowledging this helped him inquire into his anger, instead of continuing to act it out by blaming his wife. As he learned to work with his anger, the sharp energy in this emotion started to cut through his confusion, propelling him into expanded states of clarity.

In these moments of clarity Mark could see that taking his anger out on his wife was a way of diverting himself from the pain of his own paralysis. And he discovered the real cause of his stuckness: He had long ago lost touch with his soul, his own passion and vision. As a result, he had lost any deep sense of purpose or strength, and had given his wife most of the power in their relationship. Through bringing a new quality of attention to his anger and frustration, Mark found the antidote to his stuckness right at hand—in his growing awareness of what was really wrong with his life and what he needed to do to make it right. As he acknowledged both his paralysis and his longing to live more expansively, a new kind of wish was born in him—to know himself more deeply and to be more fully himself. Recognizing and honoring this holy longing roused him from his malaise and gave him a whole new sense of direction.

As a result, Mark also began to recover his long-lost desire energy in relation to his wife. In learning to recognize and express what he really wanted with her, he no longer needed to indulge in his old patterns of anger, complaint, and withdrawal.

Feeling the Tension of Opposite Pulls

An understanding of coemergence also helps clarify why we are so often attracted to lovers who push our buttons or make our lives difficult. Consider the situation of Eli, a man who found himself attracted to strong, forceful women who brought out his vulnerability—even though this was the last thing he wanted to feel, for it reminded him of the intense shame and humiliation he had suffered as a child. Why then was he drawn to women who stirred up his deepest fear?

Some would ascribe Eli's behavior to masochistic or self-destructive tendencies: "He feels unconsciously compelled to repeat his childhood, to rewound himself by continually choosing situations that prick his old sores." There is some truth in this view: The conditioned personality does tend to re-create old childhood setups, even when they are painful. But this is only half the truth. The principle of coemergence—that even apparently self-defeating behavior contains a genuine impulse hidden within it—allows us to consider the situation more deeply.

Whenever a man like Eli spends his life running away from threatening feelings, such as vulnerability, he becomes inwardly enslaved and burdened by his fear. He lives in a straitjacket, and can never relax into simply being open and present. Eli's romantic attractions were a sign that his soul wanted to break out of this cage. Though his ego sought safety, his soul wanted freedom. It drew him to women who brought him to his edge, putting him in touch with feelings that perforated his facade of indifference. A deeper intelligence within him knew that going to this edge and facing these fears was the only way he could ever truly overcome his inner burden of dread.

Instead of trying to choose between safety and freedom, the two sides of his inner tension, Eli needed to let himself *feel* this edge that his relationship with strong women brought him to. When he remained present here—where he was both attracted and repelled, intrigued and terrified—a larger reconciling awareness, above and beyond the tension of the opposites, became available. With this awareness he could see that he was excited and scared for the same reason: Something new wanted to be born in him—true confidence, which could only emerge out of coming to terms with his fear of opening himself to others.

Working with Fear and Resistance

Significant relationships always stir up this tension between the contractive tendencies of the personality and the expansive yearnings of the soul. On the soul level, I may recognize my partner's presence in my life as a call to expand and deepen my capacities to open to life more fully. But on the personality level, I may try to use her to fill my holes, so that I don't have to admit that I'm missing important pieces of myself. If I'm depressed, I may imagine: "Maybe she will cheer me up." If I'm anxious: "Maybe she will make me feel secure." In this way, my ego tries to collude with hers in building a cozy cocoon *à deux*. Instead of expanding outside my one-room flat, I try to get her to move in and help me remodel: "There's plenty of room in here—maybe we could just add an alcove or some skylights."

As long as we bring awareness to our contractive tendencies, they are not a real problem. In fact, the soul awakens only through encountering and working with the obstacles to its unfolding—the ego's tendencies to stay closed and defended. For every two steps forward we take, we often have to fall back one as we confront old resistances to moving forward. For instance, each time a couple deepen their love or grow significantly closer, they may find themselves having bigger fights than before, because all their fears and resistances are being challenged. Since openness and fear, growth and resistance to growth, always coemerge, hand in hand, we don't need to blame ourselves for this backward step. Instead, we need to meet our resistance and inquire into it.

The truth is that part of us *doesn't* want to be here—here in this moment, here in this relationship, or even here on this planet. We can't simply overcome our resistance to being present by an act of will; for the more we resist our resistance, the more divided, and less present, we become. What we *can* do is to gently surround the dark, contracted parts of ourselves with awareness. This has a profound impact: *When we feel and acknowledge our resistance to being present, we immediately become more present.* We are finally all here, no longer divided.

Fourfold Truth

Taking account of coemergence is also helpful in sorting out certain kinds of relationship conflict. When two partners fight, each of them is usually trying to convey some valid concern. However, their way of communicating this concern is often distorted by old emotional reactions and bad-Other projections. Since each person's perspective contains both a genuine and a distorted side, this means that four elements are present in most couple conflicts. I call this *fourfold truth*.

Relationship conflicts go nowhere as long as both partners focus only on their own truth and on the other's distortion, instead of recognizing the truth and distortion on *both* sides. For example, Paul and Helen would have terrible fights over her tendency to be late, because each perceived the other to be acting in a hostile way. Paul saw Helen's lateness as an expression of flagrant disregard, while Helen saw Paul's angry confrontations as mean-spirited and petty. When arguing, each of them would try in vain to make the other see the righteousness of their own side.

Helen and Paul both had a truth to convey in their conflict, though neither of them was expressing it clearly or directly. By *truth* here I mean a genuine personal concern, feeling, or desire. For Paul, punctuality was a sign of being considerate; when Helen was late, he doubted whether she really respected or cared for him. He needed to be sure of her caring, but rather than admitting this, he would go on the attack instead. This was his distortion: When she was late, he saw her as the bad Other, someone who, like his mother, discounted his needs. And the emotional intensity of his attack made it hard for Helen to hear his point of view.

Since Helen preferred to live in a looser, more relaxed way than Paul, she did not give so much importance to strict punctuality. Paul's demand that she always be on time seemed inconsiderate to her. And she felt hurt and abused by his tirades. But instead of revealing these feelings, she gave up even trying to be on time, as a way of showing him that he could not control her. This was her distortion: She too saw her partner as the bad Other, someone who, like her father, only approved of her when she did what he wanted her to do.

As long as Paul and Helen each focused only on what was right about their side and wrong about the other's, they got nowhere. What helped them overcome this impasse was recognizing that they each had valid concerns *and* that they were also conveying them in distorted ways.

Helen was able to hear Paul's concerns when he finally spoke his truth more directly, while also acknowledging his distortion: "I want to trust you, but that's hard for me when you don't seem considerate. When you're late, it touches an old sore point, where I fear that others don't respect me. So I imagine that you don't really care about me, and that makes me go on the attack. I admit that's not a good way of dealing with this." And Helen in turn was finally able to say: "It hurts me when you don't see or respect the ways I am different from you. That's what's true for me. My distortion is that I overreact when I feel that you're trying to control me. I start to see you as my father, and go out of my way to show you that you can't manipulate me." Once Paul and Helen shared their real concerns and acknowledged their distortions, their tension around this issue began to ease.

A couple's exchanges are bound to become messy when real concerns are mixed up with unconscious patterns of fear, denial, and reactivity. Acknowledging that there is truth and distortion on both sides brings clarity to the situation. Thus recognizing the truth of coemergence helps us cut through any tendency to see ourselves or our partner as all good or all bad. And this in turn brings to our relationship a much greater level of compassion and understanding.

DIALOGUE 6A

Working with Fourfold Truth

When two people are caught in a deadlock, one way to clarify the situation is by working with fourfold truth—seeing how each side contains a certain validity as well as a certain distortion. It's best to start with each partner stating his or her main concern, very simply, and then acknowledging the distorted way it has been coming across. Once two partners can acknowledge their truths *and* their distortions, the issue is no longer who is right and who is wrong, since both are right and both are wrong in different ways. This understanding reduces resentment and helps them clarify what has been going on between them.

KAREN AND DAVID

In considering the impasse between you, each of you could start by saying what's true for you. Then we'll look at how your genuine concerns become distorted in the way you communicate with each other.

> KAREN: *I feel fear, rage, and inadequacy in the area of our sexuality. I am often not sexually aroused at times when David is, and if I try, things just get worse. We've tried talking about this, but we only wind up arguing and feeling more distant. I don't understand how our bodies can react so differently. When this issue comes up, I often feel like a failure. Sometimes I think I should be a lesbian, but that's not what I really want.*

So you don't feel aroused when David is. What is happening for you at these times?

KAREN: *I'd like to be able to respond to him in a passionate, erotic way, but I often can't. I seem to want something from him that's not just physical.*

Now you're getting to your truth: You want something from him that's not just physical. What is it that you want?

KAREN: *Compassion . . . love . . . romance . . . tenderness. That's enough, isn't it?*

That is what's important to you, so that's your truth in this situation. What is your truth, David? What's your side of this?

DAVID: *I want everything to be wonderful between us, but it's not. I would like to have more freedom in the way I am sexual. It feels like she puts demands on me that are constricting. This seems like Karen's problem to me. I don't understand where I come into it. I feel a lot of frustration, as well as fear that we could break up over this.*

Maybe this seems like her problem, but let's look at your side of it right now. You say you want to feel a greater sense of freedom and spontaneity in your sexual relationship. Is that it?

DAVID: *I want to be free to be myself in my sexual expression. Sometimes Karen wants intimacy but doesn't want intercourse. And I have trouble stopping halfway.*

Karen wants sex to go hand in hand with other qualities, such as love and tenderness. Do you feel that having to express these feelings takes away your spontaneity?

DAVID: *Often at the end of the day I have a hard time summoning up those feelings.*

You want to be sexual without having to fabricate feelings you aren't experiencing. That's understandable.

But what is it you really want? What would your ideal sexual relationship look like?

DAVID: *It would be free.*

What would this freedom look like to you? How does her desire for tenderness or romance take away your freedom?

DAVID: *It's confusing for me.*

What's so confusing?

DAVID: *When someone asks me for something, I feel I have to please them.*

You don't always want to have to please Karen. You want to express your own freedom and energy. You don't want sexuality to be tied up with pleasing your partner.

DAVID: *I guess so . . .*

You seem to be having a hard time owning this truth. Are you trying to please someone?

DAVID: *Probably my mother.*

Maybe your experience as a child was that expressing your truth meant displeasing her.

DAVID: *I don't think I even knew what my truth was, because I was so concerned with pleasing her.*

So when you hear Karen say that she wants greater intimacy, what goes on for you?

DAVID: *I hear what she wants. But when I try to do something about that, it doesn't work.*

It sounds like part of you is trying to please her, while another part of you is rebelling against that. And that inner struggle makes it hard for you to respond to her in a free, spontaneous way.

DAVID: *Yes, I don't want sexuality to be all mixed up with having to please.*

That's your truth.

KAREN: *I didn't know that.*

Right. Well, *he* didn't know that either... until just now.

Next we could look at the distortions on each side.

(To Karen) When you express your desire to feel close when you make love, David can hear that. But there's probably something else happening for you here—something that prevents you from expressing this desire in a way that inspires him to respond to it. Do you have any idea what that might be?

KAREN: *I think I have some doubt about myself as a woman with a man. I know I could get what I want from another woman, but it's hard with a man.*

Is it hard for you to express your desires to a man?

KAREN: *Sometimes I don't know what I'm really asking for. I feel so needy, and I don't think that's fair to him.*

Maybe it's hard to put out your desire clearly when you feel so needy.

KAREN: *I want to feel that I'm all-important to David, that I'm cared for, loved, desired. But that also seems like asking for too much. Then I feel like I'm at war with myself, as though me and my body are going in two different directions. (crying) And then I just go numb.*

You want love and tenderness—that's real. But the distortion is that you judge that desire—which disconnects you from your body, from yourself.

KAREN: *And then I feel even more needy. And I start wanting David to be different.*

You think that if David were different, then you wouldn't become so needy or disconnect from your body. You expect him to make things right for you, or to help you stay connected with yourself. *That's* the distortion, because no one can do that for you. And it puts extra pressure on the situation.

(To David) What is it like for you to hear her acknowledge that she has all these judgments about her needs, that she disconnects from her body, and that she wants you to help her reconnect?

DAVID: *It gives me a different perspective on what is going on for her.*

How does that feel?

DAVID: *I'm not so defensive right now. Things feel softer.*

Good. Now let's see if there is some distortion in the way you express your desire for freedom and spontaneity in your sexuality.

DAVID: *Well I was brought up to please, and I'm carrying a lot of old resentment about that. Maybe I resist giving Karen what she wants because I'm so resentful about having to please. I guess I don't know the difference between genuine giving and trying to please.*

Yes. Could you try telling Karen about that?

DAVID: *Karen, I know that this is my stuff, but . . . it's hard to respond to your need for intimacy when I feel that I have to please you. That closes me right down; I disconnect from my body too.*

KAREN: *I thought I was the one who always had to please people. . . . Yes, I do expect you to make me feel comfortable with sex, and I guess that's my distortion—putting that expectation on you. I can see how that's a burden for you.*

How are you feeling right now, David?

DAVID: *I feel good about this. I feel like I made a small step here.*

Small steps add up.

KAREN: *As long as you're making them, I'm fine. . . . Oh oh, I did it again, didn't I?* (laughter)

Yes, there it is again—the truth and the distortion coming up together. You want him to be more present in a loving way—that's your truth. But you also make that into an expectation. The sense of humor is important here: "Oh oh, I did it again, didn't I?" That's a way of being gentle with yourself when you see this tendency come up.

DAVID: *There's something here that still feels confusing. I can understand Karen's desire for me to be more emotionally sensitive and tender. But there is something in me as a male that is not emotional and tender. Sometimes I feel just a raw physical lust. It's usually hard to say this because I'm afraid she might think I'm a boor, a son of a bitch. Or she might run away. Sometimes I just have this strong physical urge that is not just soft and sweet.*

KAREN: *Well, I can handle that sometimes.*

DAVID: *You can? But I thought you wanted me to be all soft and tender. . . .*

KAREN: *What I want is to feel connected with you when we make love.*

You can only feel connected with each other sexually when you each feel connected with yourselves.

(To David) When you expressed your desire for raw sexuality as you did just now—totally, energetically, unapologetically—Karen could respond to that because you *were* so connected and present! That's what is most important here—not whether you are tender and romantic all the time.

In this exchange we can see how David and Karen's sexual difficulty is a teacher for them by calling on them to be more present and real, both with themselves and with each other. Karen's truth is that she wants David to be more present—to be there with her more fully—when they make love. And when she lets him know that, it forces him to deal with what keeps him from being present—his conflict about needing to please. David's truth is that he wants their lovemaking to be more spontaneous. And when he expresses that, it forces Karen to deal with what keeps her from being present—her tendency to get caught up in judgments of herself and expectations of him. So each person's genuine desire calls on the other to be more authentic as well.

At the same time, the distortions each of them brings to the sexual arena also trigger the other's distortion. Karen's judgments and expectations activate David's resentment about having to please, and that makes it hard for him to stay present. And that in turn leaves her feeling more needy, judgmental, and demanding. In this way, their struggle becomes a vicious circle, in which each person's inner conflict keeps stirring up the other's.

When two partners trigger each other's distortions like this, it is hard for them to see clearly what is going on. These are the times when working with fourfold truth—acknowledging both their genuine concerns *and* their distortions—can help a couple sort out what is happening, in a nonadversarial way. In doing this, Karen and David have started to clarify that they both want the same thing, underneath their opposing positions—to be more fully present in their lovemaking.

Chapter Seven

CHAOS AND NEW BIRTH

*Nothing in the world can change from one reality
into another unless it first turns into nothing, that is,
into the reality of the between-stage. And then it is
made into a new creature, from the egg to the chick.
The moment when the egg is no more and the chick
is not yet, is nothingness. This is the primal state
which no one can grasp because it is a force which
precedes creation; it is called chaos.*

FROM *Tales of the Hasidim*
MARTIN BUBER

Chaos should be regarded as extremely good news.
CHÖGYAM TRUNGPA

If love is like a sun whose radiant warmth causes us to
stir and expand inside the seed husk of our conditioned
personality, then as this protective shell starts to crack
open, we are bound to experience moments of uncertainty
or panic. For even though our old identities impede our

development, they do provide a certain comfort and security. When one of them starts to dissolve, it often seems as though our orderly world is falling into chaos.

In moments when an old defensive facade begins to crack, but we have not yet found a new way of being to take its place, we experience what the Hasidic sage quoted above calls the "between-stage"—where "the egg is no more and the chick is not yet." Although this in-between state may seem threatening, it also provides a special opportunity to let go of what has gone before and reorient ourselves to the new situation at hand. Therefore, it is important to learn how to move through these times of uncertainty and upheaval, for they can lead to significant new beginnings—to new birth, as the sage suggests.

Anna was a competent "self-made woman" in her early forties, who had survived a difficult family situation, put herself through college and business school, and become a high-level corporate manager through the force of her own drive and intelligence. She had been married and divorced twice, but only now, for the first time, was she experiencing how sweet love could be. She had finally met a man to whom her soul responded with an unqualified yes.

Precisely because Anna felt so open to Sean, she also experienced tremendous doubt and insecurity. Fearing that his reluctance to rush into marriage could lead to abandonment or emotional ruin, she tried to pressure him into a commitment he was not ready for. When that didn't work, she was at a loss. She had emerged halfway from behind her cool, competent facade, yet to continue feeling so exposed completely terrified her.

The chaos in her mind and body became so intense that she bolted, announcing to Sean that the relationship was over. Two weeks later, overwhelmed with pain, she called me for counseling. The following condensed description of her work with me brings together, in sum-mary form, the major themes discussed in this book so far; it also illustrates a method for moving through the emotional chaos that arises as we let go of old identities, on the way toward recovering lost dimensions of our being.

Inquiring into Emotional Reactions

The first step in moving through this kind of chaos is to inquire into our highly charged reactions, to find out what is giving rise to them. In Anna's case, her flight reaction arose out of her panic about feeling so open with a man who was unsure of his intentions toward her. Sean's uncertainty was natural, given the lingering hurt he still felt from a marriage that had recently ended. Although Anna understood this rationally, she still felt threatened and terrified.

In exploring her flight reaction, Anna found that what really upset her, even more than losing Sean, was the emergence of a painful unconscious identity—a sense of herself as a forlorn child, whom no one would ever love because her need was too great. All her life she had covered this abyss with trance: She had fled this needy-child identity by trying to make herself into Superwoman—someone who was totally controlled and competent in the affairs of life, and who had no pressing emotional needs. But now that her desire for real love had emerged, her conscious identity as Superwoman was in danger of collapsing, and her unconscious identity as a desperate child threatened to overwhelm her.

Exploring the Felt Sense

Since every self-image is maintained by old stories—beliefs we tell ourselves about "how reality is"—bringing these to light is an essential step in loosening an identity's grip. The central story behind Anna's needy-child identity was: "I don't trust that anyone could ever *really* see me or love me." As long as she believed that love was untrustworthy, and that she also was unworthy of it, she prevented herself from receiving the only thing that could dissolve her distrust—love itself.

When Anna realized that her distrust was part of a story she told herself, rather than an accurate appraisal of reality, she was ready to take the next step—directly facing this distrust. I encouraged her to see how it felt in her body, and to let it be there, without judgment or opposition. This put her in touch with what psychologist Eugene Gendlin calls a *felt sense*—a bodily-felt sensation, with its own particular feeling-tone and texture. When we gently explore a felt sense, without putting a preconceived interpretation on it, it can reveal important information about what is going on inside us that is not otherwise available to the rational mind.

As Anna faced her distrust, she experienced it as an empty, aching sensation in her belly. This hollow, dry ache did not have the same emotional intensity as her initial panic, but it was a deeper, more significant feeling. Ever since childhood she had known this sense of emptiness, where she imagined she lacked real substance. This was her abyss—what she was really running away from when she tried to break off the relationship with Sean. Since she had built a whole life around avoiding this feeling, it had become the central hub around which all the pretenses and distractions of her life revolved.

Sitting with the hollow feeling in her belly, Anna realized just how unnourished she felt inside. As a child, she had summoned all her strength to rise above the emotional neglect in her family and go on living. And she had prevailed—she was a highly accomplished woman. Yet to succeed at this, she had had to deny her underlying sense of emptiness and deprivation. Now that her love for Sean had expanded her awareness and sensitivity, she could no longer avoid facing what stood in the way of her further expansion. In order to be fully present and available to someone she loved, she would have to face and deal with her fear of being nothing, and its associated feelings of hunger, shame, deficiency, and distrust.

On the Edge of the Abyss

Encountering threatening feelings that have long been concealed behind a facade brings us to the edge of our abyss, where we start to enter unknown territory. As Anna sat on this edge, her inner demons cried out: "You'd better not go near this emptiness. If you do, it will swallow you alive. Then your worst fear will come true—you'll find you really don't exist after all."

Feeling the pain, fear, or emptiness we have spent our whole life avoiding is the last thing in the world any of us would ever want to do. At this point it helps to recognize our flight from these feelings as an old childhood defense, based on the child's belief: "This feeling is bigger than I am. If I feel this, it could destroy me." That may have been true for us as children, when our nervous system was too delicate to handle intensely painful feelings, especially in the absence of support and guidance from the adult world. *But it is no longer the case.*

The more we keep such feelings shut away in the dark, the more they remain a festering wound in our psyche, which we have to spend huge amounts of energy avoiding or concealing. We wind up living a lie, as Anna did by pretending to be Superwoman, while doubting herself underneath. If we want to free ourselves from this kind of exhausting charade, *we have to be willing to open to the feeling we least want to feel.* We need to experience our suffering consciously, at last. This is very different from wallowing in it—tormenting ourselves with painful thoughts and stories. It requires an active yet relaxed quality of presence.

Recovering Lost Being

When we finally open to our pain, giving it plenty of space instead of trying to stuff it away in a dark corner, it never turns out to be as scary or overwhelming as we imagined. This discovery—that we can in fact tolerate the dreaded anger, fear, sorrow, or emptiness we have been denying— allows us to make friends with our experience and relax into ourselves in a new way. It develops and expands our capacity to be authentically present.

All these years Anna had fled from her empty feelings because she thought that they indicated something terribly wrong with her, and that they would swallow her up like a black hole if she faced them. Yet as she learned to acknowledge and allow her emptiness, without buying into old stories about it, she found that she didn't disappear after all. On the contrary, through being willing to experience her abyss—that place where she had lost touch with her own substance and value—she became more present and connected with herself.

This did not happen right away; we had to come back to the sense of hollowness many times before Anna could stay present there, without dissociating or going numb. An important turning point was her discovery of a deep desire for love at the core of her emptiness. As Anna acknowledged that love was more important to her than all her facades and defenses, the emptiness no longer seemed so scary; it became more spacious and tranquil, like a deep, starry sky. Through confronting the feeling she feared most, Anna had begun to come alive in the place inside where she had gone dead.

This is what usually happens when we finally stand our ground and face the abyss we have been trying to avoid all our life. If we continue to run from it, it remains a dead spot in the psyche where the warmth of human presence is absent. And it perpetuates a sense of deficiency, a haunting belief that there really *is* something wrong with us.

The truth is that we feel empty inside not because we are deficient, but because we are cut off from the fullness of our own being. We are never *truly* impoverished, because our true nature—the "wish-fulfilling gem" that contains all the resources we need—is always with us. "You can never lose what belongs to you, even if you throw it away," as the ancient Chinese book of wisdom, *I Ching*, counsels. But until we discover that we are still alive and well in that place where we once, long ago, gave up on ourselves, we may never come to realize this.

Genuine Sadness and Longing

In recognizing how cut off from herself she had been all these years, Anna felt great sorrow. This kind of sadness always contains tremendous intelligence. It is the cry of the soul, in response to having been trapped for so long in a mistaken identity. If we can open to this sadness, it puts us directly in touch with our soul. And this yields an unexpected blessing that can turn our life around: a genuine desire to live in a whole new way.

Realizing that her own self-rejection had been the cause of her hunger and emptiness was, for Anna, like finding the key to unlock her prison door. Out of this realization a new desire arose within her—to treat herself kindly and let herself be nourished. Just acknowledging this desire began to put her in touch with the kindness and nourishment already present within her. She felt a sense of warmth and support flowing into her belly, where the dry ache had been.

In the Hasidic metaphor, Anna's conscious identity as Superwoman was the shell that had to break open before she could be "made into a new creature." On the way, she had to pass through the chaos of the "between-stage," where she confronted the dreaded identity she had always run from—seeing herself as a deficient child. The "new creature" born here was a depth of soul, an inner warmth and vitality, which was, in another sense, nothing "new" at all. It was the source of inner nourishment she had lost touch with long ago.

Tapping into this inner source helped Anna open up to Sean again, and to feel nourished by his love, despite her uncertainty about his long-term intentions. This had a powerful impact on him. Previously she had pushed for future commitment without letting herself receive his love in the present—a confusing and disturbing situation for him. But now that she was finally letting in his love, he found himself drawn to her in a new way.

Fullness of Being

Anna's journey shows how we can use the chaotic emotions arising in relationships as entry points into a deeper connection with ourselves and our partner. The first step is to look underneath our reactions for the self-image triggering them, and see the stories and beliefs holding this identity in place. Then we need to acknowledge the feelings that have been hidden by this identity. That will usually bring us to the edge of our abyss, where we encounter a sense of fear, uncertainty, or loss that we have been denying and avoiding for a long time.

The next step is to face this abyss, where we have lost access to some essential aspect of our being—our wisdom, our strength, our basic goodness. Our willingness to remain open and present here brings about a softening, which acts like a solvent on the hardened structure of the old identity. Like ice dissolving into its true nature as water, our rigid facade starts to melt, revealing the open, responsive quality of aliveness it had been constricting. This meltdown is what the soul most wants from love—to know itself again as a living presence, no longer trapped in the confines of conditioned setups from the past.

So even when we feel most cut off or dead inside, we can regain access to the nourishing qualities of our being *by staying present with the feeling of their absence*. Experiencing our lack of strength, for instance, takes strength, and thus activates strength. Facing our lack of courage is courageous. Acknowledging our lack of compassion and generosity is compassionate and generous. In opening to the truth of our present experience, no matter how painful it seems to be, we start to reconnect with ourselves in a place where we have been disconnected.

Here is where relationship can be such a powerful teacher: By bringing us up against the boundaries of where we fear to tread, it helps us learn to become present in the places where we've been most absent. Love's challenges propel us toward discovering what we most need in order to be true to ourselves and our partner—the lost fullness of our being. Gaining access to this powerful presence within us is what will allow us to handle whatever situation comes along. This is the only true and lasting resolution to the difficulties we face in our lives and our relationships.

Chapter Eight

LEAD INTO GOLD

Negativity clearly seen becomes intelligence.
Chögyam Trungpa

As two people's love for each other penetrates their hardened defenses, it brings to light hidden negativities—raw edges in themselves and in their relationship that they would rather keep hidden away in the dark. When we live alone, we develop strategies for ignoring these raw edges. But when we live with someone we love, we can no longer hide from ourselves like this.

It is important to let these negativities come out into the open, where we can work with them in the light of awareness and compassion. Only then can they relax their anxious grip, yielding access to hidden resources they have been blocking. If we always try to avoid the darker aspects of ourselves, they remain underground, and never evolve in a more positive direction. Even worse, they start to fester and spread, eventually contaminating our whole relationship or our whole life, like poison seeping into groundwater. Learning to work directly with negativity is an essential step on the path of conscious relationship.

Negative Negativity

Often when our shadow side comes to light, we criticize ourselves or our partner for bringing out the worst in us. Yet blame is just another form of negativity, which only aggravates the situation.

Whenever we turn against something negative in ourselves or our partner, we are essentially contracting against a contraction, effectively tightening the knot rather than letting it unravel. In fact, our aversion to a negative feeling often contains, and thus intensifies, the very quality we are trying to push away. Censuring our anger, for instance, is a further act of aggression. Denying our fear is a further expression of fear. Blaming ourselves for being stingy is ungenerous and only makes us hold on more tightly. Like Brer Rabbit's attacks on the Tar-Baby in the Uncle Remus story, our aversive reactions to our dark side keep us stuck in the very tendencies that cause us the most pain. That is why Chögyam Trungpa once called this kind of reaction "negative negativity."

Working with Negativity

Often what keeps us from acknowledging our negative tendencies is a fear of being judged for them. Perhaps we imagine our partner will no longer respect us if we reveal our flaws or limitations. But this is usually a projection: We are seeing our own critic—the part of ourselves that condemns us for being human, all too human—in our partner's eyes. Before we can work creatively with negativity, we must first learn to neutralize the attacks of our inner critic.

As a step in this direction, it is important to make a crucial distinction—between *discernment* and *condemnation*. We need to be able to *discern* whatever truth there is in the critic's message—which may be trying to tell us where we are off the mark—while putting aside the tendency to *condemn* ourselves for our failings. This means learning to stand up to the critic's attack—firmly saying "no" to its censure—while at the same time recognizing what it is trying to bring to our attention: "Yes, it's true . . . I am often lost and out of touch . . . I try to use my partner to fill up my holes and shore up my ego . . . I have a hard time really listening . . . when I give, I am often looking for something in return . . ." When we can gently admit to ourselves where we are off track, we take away the critic's ammunition.

If contracting against negativity only creates more negativity, the opposite is also true—acknowledging it diminishes its power, revealing positive impulses concealed within it. For example, perhaps your relationship brings to light your tendency to be selfish. If you attack yourself for this, then it only goes underground, becoming more furtive and entrenched. What's needed instead is a deeper understanding of the selfishness—what it consists of and where it comes from. In truth, you probably don't know why you are selfish, or even what this "selfishness" really is. You may have theories about it, but you have probably never looked into it that deeply. And it will never really change or evolve until you do.

The key, once again, lies in allowing and inquiry. Allowing does not mean acting out impulses. Instead, it means letting your experience be there, just as it is, and touching it directly. Both the allowing and the touch should be gentle. This takes practice, steadfastness, and courage.

When you let yourself experience the selfish impulse as it arises—noticing how it feels in your body—you may find a certain sensation connected with it, perhaps a tightness in the belly or chest. Looking further, you see that this contraction indicates something inside you desperately trying to hold on; and that underneath this grasping there is a tremendous hunger. In acknowledging this, you may find the tightness starting to ease. Then if you explore the underlying sense of hunger, to see where it's coming from, you may realize that you are not very generous with yourself—which creates an inner sense of poverty. As a result, you always try to "get what's coming to you."

In recognizing your grasping as an attempt to remedy a sense of poverty, you start to bring compassionate understanding to what is going on inside you, instead of simply condemning it and remaining divided against yourself. Then you can also address the real issue—the need to be more generous with yourself—instead of unconsciously acting it out through selfish behavior.

Even though negative tendencies do not always open up like this right away, they eventually will if we keep inquiring into them, without blame. All negativity is the result of some loss of being. When we discover how we are disconnected from ourselves, we see our negativity for what it really is—a cry for attention from some part of us we've forgotten, which we can only recover once we recognize it's been lost.

Bringing the Relationship Shadow out into the Open

Just as every individual develops an unconscious shadow—an array of denied feelings, perceptions, and responses that do not fit an idealized self-image—so every couple develops a relationship shadow. Robert Bly once likened the shadow to a long bag, stuffed with unwanted experiences, that weighs us down as we drag it around with us. Relationships also become weighed down by their shadow—all the denials, evasions, resentments, and grievances that a couple have stuffed away over many months or years.

As two partners' grievances accumulate, they become increasingly afraid to open up the bag, for fear that their relationship will be swept away in a torrent of negativity. As a result, the bag grows heavier and the distance between them increases, while symptoms of their accumulated bad feelings—distrust and resentment, withdrawal and distancing, loss of sexual interest, excessive harshness and lack of forgiveness—start poisoning the atmosphere.

Couples can never entirely avoid accumulating this kind of shadow. Even in the most conscious of relationships, tensions and frictions are bound to build up. Often the more loving two people feel, the less inclined they are to focus on areas of conflict. Therefore couples need to practice consciously emptying the bag on occasion, by setting aside special times to explore grievances and resentments that have been building under the surface.

According to the principle of coemergence discussed in chapter six, all forms of negativity contain a certain intelligence. So if two people can talk over their negative feelings in a spirit of openness and caring, they will also uncover important messages that need to be communicated, for their own well-being and for the good of their relationship. And when they realize that it is possible to reveal what they thought they had to hide, this builds trust and strengthens the relationship as a container or "holding environment" where all the different parts of themselves can be included.

This kind of airing, which seems so threatening at first, revives the spark that was dampened by denial and evasion, freeing up a flow of positive energy between them.

And as their love comes back, it feels especially sweet, like fresh air after a storm.

Turning a Weak Link into a Strong Link

In addition to working with negativity in ourselves and our relationships, we need to learn how to relate to the less evolved parts of our partner as well. How do we deal with what we most dislike in those we love—their fear, their rigidities, their low self-esteem, their depression, their anger, their blind spots? Often we try to wage a crusade against these negative elements. Or we ignore them and hope for the best. Or else we resign ourselves, suffer in silence, and think about leaving.

The place where lovers rub up against each other's rough edges is usually the weak link in their relationship. Here is where their bond most easily starts to fray and unravel. Yet this is also where their love is really put to the test. If they can learn to relate more consciously to each other's negative tendencies, they may find themselves reaping unexpected benefits.

For one person, this might involve standing up and saying no to a judgmental tendency in her partner—which may help her find hidden strength in herself. This leads to greater self-respect, which may in turn help her partner respect her more as well. For another person, it may be important to learn to treat her partner's inner conflicts with loving-kindness—which expands her own capacity for love, while also developing a deeper level of trust and friendship between them. And for another, relating to what troubles him in his partner may force him to come to terms with parts of himself he has never acknowledged before. For instance, if his partner has a tendency to feel sad or depressed, this may threaten him because he has always run away from his own weightier feelings. Learning to relate to this side of his partner helps him connect with his own darker, deeper soul qualities, bringing him down to earth from his boyish illusions of life as an eternal, Icarus-like ascent.

Being Each Other's Teacher

No friend, therapist, or spiritual teacher could ever feel the impact of my negative tendencies as vividly as my partner does. And no one else could ever have as much interest in seeing her open or expand in places where she is contracted as I do. So if we both want to grow in these areas, it would be wise to enlist each other's aid. Having a soul connection means that each can ask the other for support or guidance in areas where the other is stronger or more evolved.

A couple wanting to explore this might start by asking themselves, "Am I willing to receive help from my partner with this part of myself that I have a hard time with? And am I willing to extend the same kind of help to her (him)?" If they have this willingness, they could then formally ask each other for support or guidance in an area of difficulty, and let each other know what would be most helpful.

For example, a man who has difficulty residing in his heart or revealing his feelings might ask his partner for help with this, if this is one of her strengths. He might also let her know what would help him most; for instance: "It's not helpful if you lecture me or become disapproving when my heart is closed. It would help me most if you could hear my struggle with this, share your knowledge or understanding in this area, and provide encouragement."

Conversely, when those we love ask for our help with one of their weak points, this provides an opportunity to relate to this part of them in a more conscious, empowered way, instead of just putting up with it. Here we will find that our work on learning to be present with our own raw edges is the best practice we could have for helping those we love. What will help them most is no different from what we ourselves need when we feel stuck: Instead of trying to fix them, we can give them space, let them have their experience, and be there for them, maintaining presence and friendly contact.

As two partners learn to be there for each other in this way, their soul connection deepens, and their areas of weakness become a source of unexpected strength.

Chapter Nine

THE POWER OF
TRUTH-TELLING

A couple's ability to work consciously with their rough edges and frictions breaks down when they fall into a certain kind of unproductive, repetitious wrangling, which we might call their "Argument." This is a seemingly endless series of skirmishes around a central issue, with countless installments and variations, going round and round without ever reaching resolution.

Some relationship conflict, as discussed earlier, can become a kind of sacred combat, as it penetrates our facades and challenges us to be more authentically present. Other kinds of conflict also serve a positive function by compelling a couple to address problem areas they have denied or ignored. By contrast, the Argument that keeps recurring—in the form of ongoing bickering, guerilla sniping, or emotional blow-ups—leaves two partners feeling misunderstood, discouraged, and drained. We have already seen how old self/Other setups from childhood are at the root of this kind of conflict; here we will focus on how two people can cut through it and put it to rest.

There is a simple reason why couples usually cannot resolve their Argument: They are not addressing the real issue. They *think* that the issue is some difference between them—their opposite ways of handling money, managing household affairs, expressing their feelings, or relating to their sexuality. This is rarely the main problem. Two people can always find a way to work out, or at least live with, their differences if they really want to. The real issue is how their disagreements touch old sensitivities inside each of them—where they feel vulnerable, uncertain, isolated, or afraid. As the Argument proceeds, it keeps irritating these sensitivities, until the whole area of discussion feels like a huge bruise.

If two partners do not know how to talk about the underlying sensitivities that their conflict inflames—or even *whether* they could talk about such things—they will never be able to address the deeper issue that keeps fueling their Argument. And consequently, it will never be resolved. Instead they will continue to wrangle over the false issue: *who is doing what to whom.*

Cutting Through the Argument

To cut through the Argument, two people need to learn how to talk about their raw edges with each other, instead of focusing so narrowly on the content of their disagreement. This kind of conversation is essential in developing a more conscious relationship. According to psychologist James Hillman, consciousness involves "maintaining conversation," while unconsciousness involves "letting things fall out of conversation." Consider your family of origin: Certain issues that were never talked about turned into demons haunting the family because no one could acknowledge them. Similarly, when our concerns fall out of conversation in a relationship—hurts and grudges we're holding on to, doubts and fears that our partner stirs up in us, desires we are afraid to admit——they live concealed in the shadows. And from there they return to haunt us, in the form of this senseless Argument that goes nowhere.

So it is essential for couples to learn how to have conversations they never thought they could have——about what is really happening inside them. Intimate conversation is a venture and an inquiry. It involves taking risks—— by revealing what's going on inside us, behind our facades. This opens up new possibilities between two people, allowing them to connect on a much deeper level.

Gale and Patrick had been dating for a year. Their Argument centered around the issue of monogamy. Patrick wanted to be free to see other women occasionally, while Gale needed a more committed relationship. Whenever they argued about this, each of them wound up feeling misunderstood, hurt, and manipulated by the other.

When I first asked Patrick what was happening for him, he could only say, "This is what I want to do. I won't have anyone telling me how to live my life." But as he explored further what was going on for him, he realized that he was afraid of being trapped. Whenever he sensed a restriction on his freedom, he felt as if his very survival were at stake. And then he would have to prove to his partner that he remained free, by seeing other women. He had already destroyed two marriages this way.

Thus the question of monogamy touched on a much deeper issue for Patrick. His father had been ruthlessly domineering, always telling him what to do. And whenever he wanted to do things his own way, his father criticized him for being selfish. As he saw how this dynamic with his father played itself out inside him, Patrick began to realize that monogamy was not the real issue, but only the content of the Argument.

The real question for Patrick was how to deal with two warring voices inside him: the internalized parent always telling him what to do and the rebellious adolescent always having to prove he could do whatever he damn well pleased. Neither of these sides had ever brought him happiness or fulfillment, and their struggle inside him only tore him apart. In seeing all this, Patrick had taken the first step in cutting through the Argument—looking within himself and uncovering the deeper underlying concern.

Truth-Telling as Self-Revelation

The next step involves revealing to our partner the truth about what is really going on inside us. The Argument is like an onstage sparring match between two egos who are mainly interested in defending themselves and looking good. The best way to end this kind of power struggle is to invite our partner to step out of the stage lights and come around backstage with us. When two people let each other in on what is going on behind the scenes, they start to forge a deeper, sympathetic bond. And this is what will help them put a stop to the sparring between their egos.

At first it was hard for Patrick to reveal what he was struggling with. Like many men, he thought that his inner feelings weren't of much interest or significance. Therefore how could talking about them help resolve his conflict with Gale? It surprised him to learn that knowing what went on inside him was of real interest to her, and that it was the key to helping her understand his behavior and attitudes, which otherwise seemed inexplicable to her.

When Patrick let Gale in on the painful struggle going on behind his defiant facade, her first response was, "I never heard you say anything like that before." She felt relieved that he'd finally begun sharing his struggle with her, letting her in on what was going on for him, instead of keeping it locked away inside. She also felt some compassion for what he was dealing with. Gale's feelings of empathy and relief were not surprising; most people respond this way when those they love openly share their deepest concerns.

Having responded with empathy at first, Gale then began to tighten up as she launched into her side of the Argument: "But I can't handle your seeing other women. I won't stand for it. . . . " Then I asked her to do what Patrick had done—to see what sensitivity their disagreement touched in her.

Gale had grown up as a tomboy in a hard-core inner-city neighborhood where kids were often threatened, even knifed in the halls of her school. As a result, she had developed a tough facade, behind which she felt frightened and insecure. The monogamy Argument touched this raw, vulnerable place in her that she rarely let anyone see.

So for Gale too there were deeper issues underlying the Argument about monogamy: If she let down her guard, if she felt and revealed her feminine softness, could she survive in this world? Could she share her sensitivity with a man and trust that he would not take advantage of her?

When Gale felt vulnerable, her usual strategy was to fortify herself by attacking Patrick: "What's the matter with you? . . . You always want your own way . . . You're not trustworthy . . . I can't count on you. . . . " Though we often characterize our partner in such negative ways in the heat of the Argument, this is one of the most counterproductive things we can do. It triggers our partner's reactivity, throwing him or her into a defensive trance. When Gail would attack, Patrick would see her as the bad Other—the controlling parent out to shame and admonish him. This would stir up panic and provoke his defiance, which only created more distance between them.

Now, with my encouragement, Gail was able to take a different tack. She started to let Patrick in on her inner reality: "I've had to be tough ever since I was a kid. I have tremendous fear about letting down my guard and being soft or vulnerable with you. I'm terrified about being hurt and taken advantage of." Responding that this was the first time she had ever told him this, Patrick visibly softened, reaching out to hold her hand.

To their surprise, Patrick and Gale realized that they were in a similar situation. This is what often happens when two people bring to light the deeper issues underlying their Argument: They find common ground where they had previously been at odds. In their different ways, each of them felt that intimate relationship threatened their emotional survival. They both had a central need that the other did not seem to recognize: for Patrick, his need to feel autonomous, and for Gale, her need to feel safe about opening and softening. And they each felt vitally threatened when they thought the other did not respect this core need.

When I asked Patrick how he felt at this point, he said, "I don't know . . . kind of discombobulated." Now that he had shared his struggle with Gale and softened toward her, he was at loose ends. With nothing to rebel against, his usual defense strategy became obsolete. This brought him to a new edge.

Not feeling comfortable there, Patrick's first impulse was to ask, "Okay, now what do we do? What's the answer?" I understood that he wanted to jump off the razor's edge because it felt unsafe to be so disarmed. But I also wanted him to feel what it was like to remain present and open at this new juncture. I said, "It's too soon for solutions. Usually you have all your angles and strategies worked out. Can you just see what it's like instead to be in this place where you're unsure of what to do? If you can let yourself stay present here, perhaps the next step will reveal itself organically."

After a long pause, Patrick said, "You know, I really don't trust that I can be in a relationship and still have myself." As he acknowledged this distrust, and saw how it permeated his whole life, he grew more animated. Raising both arms, he exclaimed, "I've never really had that." "What would it be like to be in a relationship and still have yourself?" I asked. He sat back in his chair, breathed a sigh, and after a while, said, "Free . . . lots of space . . . I could just relax . . . It would be great!" In recognizing how important it was for him not to lose himself with someone he loved, Patrick was acknowledging the deeper truth underneath his desire to see other women. As a result, this desire became much less insistent.

Gale also arrived at a new edge by remaining present in her place of uncertainty, where she doubted she could trust anyone enough to let down her guard. And this led her to acknowledge *her* deep truth: She wanted to be able to soften in love, without being destroyed.

How interesting that Patrick and Gale had each chosen a partner who would bring them to an edge where their old defensive strategies no longer worked and they had to dive deeper to find out what they really wanted. There was obviously something important to keep exploring here. Revealing their core sensitivities to each other had been a vulnerable unmasking that brought them closer, so that they no longer felt compelled to fight so desperately for their *positions*. This shift provided a completely new context for discussing the issue of monogamy.

In the course of their negotiations on the monogamy issue, they found themselves continually having to go beyond what they had thought possible, both in communicating their different truths and in trying to understand each other. In this way, the very issue that had divided them became a vehicle for greater intimacy. It was clear that even if they did not ultimately stay together, their conflict had helped each of them expand and develop in significant new ways.

Exposing the Raw Edge

Conventional social relations are built on maintaining facades, defending an image, appearing to be someone we're not. This is the hallmark of unconscious relationship—one based on self-concealment and self-defense. *A conscious relationship,* by contrast, *thrives on self-revelation.* A soul connection can grow and deepen only when two people take the risk of letting down their facades and revealing themselves as they are.

Usually we are afraid to expose our raw edges, where we feel vulnerable, uncertain, or less than perfect. Imagining that our sore points indicate something wrong with us, we fear that they will be used against us if we expose them. So we try to hide them and put on our best face, especially in the early stages of a relationship.

Eventually, however, the need to be real, to be ourselves, calls on us to be honest about our inner experience, wounds and all. Exposing a raw edge should not be mistaken for wallowing in our pain or making an exhibitionistic display of our psychic damage. That is usually a form of manipulation. Genuine self-disclosure, by contrast, feels tender and tentative. Such moments can be occasions for deep healing—when we discover that we can be ourselves with someone we love, and that this actually strengthens the bond between us.

Usually we have this all backward: We are ashamed of our raw edges and imagine that no one could love us if they saw them. We believe that exposing them is a sign of weakness, so we try to hide them and pretend they don't exist. That may be appropriate behavior for a military battlefield. But in an intimate relationship the reverse holds true: Revealing our inner experience is a sign of strength, one of the most courageous things we can do.

This doesn't mean that we always have to go around baring our soul or taking ourselves seriously. Instead, as two partners learn to reveal the humanness behind their facades, this fosters a sense of humor that can help them move through difficult impasses in their relationship. To say too much about humor, much less to try to prescribe it, would be to rob it of the spontaneity that is its very essence. Yet in my own marriage, I must say that the wild card of outrageous silliness—whose impromptu arrival on the scene always leavens the weighty matters at hand—has sometimes helped us move through tense and difficult moments as powerfully as any formal communication skill. Even great bodhisattvas, whose noble mission in the Buddhist tradition is to serve all sentient beings, have been known to fail at their task because they lacked a sense of humor.

No-Fault Listening

What kills both humor and self-disclosure is blame. Therefore, it is important for two partners to agree not to use anything revealed in moments of truth-telling against each other. That is why in couples counseling, *no-fault listening* is the most important ground rule and practice. When two partners can listen to each other in a spirit of openness and good faith, sharing their inner experience helps establish a deep bond between them. They find that they are not so different after all, despite their differences. And the memory of being there for each other in their darkest and most shaky moments helps hold them together at other times, when conflict threatens to tear them apart.

Couples often imagine they need fancy communication skills or problem-solving tools to fix what has gone wrong between them. They don't realize how simple it can be *just* to tell the truth; how powerful it can be *just* to reveal their raw edges or say what they really want; and how this is often all that is needed to bring about healing, understanding, and reconciliation. One couple I met with provided an especially striking example. In the space of their first ninety-minute session they put an end to two years of recrimination and began to establish a new basis of mutual trust and respect.

When Eric and Caroline first entered my office, they were on the brink of ending their relationship, which had been eroded by two years of anger, hurt, and sexual frustration. Two years earlier Caroline revealed to Eric that she had been unfaithful to him for a brief time in their first year together. Though they'd spent countless hours talking and fighting about this incident, and working on it separately, they had not found a way to heal the rift and put it behind them.

Although this was a sophisticated couple, with a wide range of experience in psychological and spiritual work, they had not found a way to be present with each other in the pain of this conflict. Nonetheless, because of all the work they'd done on themselves, I sensed that they could, with a little guidance, get right down to essentials. Instead of delving into all the emotional complexities between them, I asked, "Would you be willing to tell each other what is going on inside you right now?"

After sifting through several layers of his pain and anger, Eric was able to find and reveal what Caroline's betrayal had touched in him, a doubt that went back to his relationship with his parents: "I'm afraid that I'm not enough for you." As he said this, he was totally exposed, totally present, totally in contact with himself and with her. Even though he had said similar things at other times, he had never done so in such an immediate, self-revealing way. Therefore this was a totally new communication, unlike anything he had ever expressed before.

Eric's recurring anger and blame had taken a tremendous toll on Caroline, who began the session feeling depressed, hopeless, and closed down inside. Yet in exposing his raw edge, Eric's words and presence were so genuine, so honest, so revealing, that she immediately perked up. For the first time in a long while, she was not on the defensive. After a long silence, during which they maintained steady eye contact, she said, "My whole body completely relaxed when you said that. Something really opened up and let go. I appreciate you for being so honest."

Then Caroline revealed her truth: "I'm terribly angry and sad about what has happened to you, to me, and to our relationship during these past two years. I keep trying to stuff down these feelings, but that only leaves me depressed. I've also been stuffing myself down in our relationship— like I did as a child when my parents couldn't appreciate who I was—because I've been afraid that you couldn't ever truly love me." These last words sent an electric charge through the room. Again, neither of them attempted to do anything about what had been said. Eric let Caroline know that he had heard her, and they sat together in silence once again, meeting each other's open gaze.

These moments of silence, which continued to arise during the rest of the session, were much more powerful than anything either of them could have done to try to fix things. It was as though they were hearing and understanding each other at a level much deeper than words. Each of them had exposed a raw edge by revealing a core truth about themselves, without any sugar coating: Eric, his fear that he was not enough, and Caroline, her fear that she couldn't be truly loved. In letting themselves have their different truths and receiving each other's disclosures with the utmost respect, they began to re-establish lovingkindness and honest presence as the ground of their connection. In this way, a deep healing took place between them. Though they still had plenty of work to do, they could now proceed in a new way.

Truth and Sacred Space

When we reveal ourselves to our partner and find that this brings healing rather than harm, we make an important discovery—that intimate relationship can provide a sanctuary from the world of facades, a sacred space where we can be ourselves, as we are. Most religions have recognized the importance of self-revelation and created a special place for it in the ritual of confession. I am not proposing that a relationship should become a confessional in any formal or religious sense. Yet it is important to understand that this kind of unmasking—speaking our truth, sharing our inner struggles, and revealing our raw edges—is sacred activity, which allows two souls to meet and touch more deeply.

If we refuse to reveal what is true for us, our connection with another will remain stuck at the personality level, and the deeper flows of vital energy will dry up. So the best way to set things right when our connection begins losing vitality is to ask ourselves, "How am I not being truthful with myself and with my partner?" Telling the truth is wonderfully restorative—the best tonic for a relationship that there is.

DIALOGUE 9A

No-Fault Listening:
Speaking and Hearing the Truth

A couple's Argument will never lead anywhere as long as they focus on scoring points or proving themselves right, while failing to address the deeper underlying issues. The best way to bring such issues into the open is by creating a *no-fault listening zone* where you and your partner can take turns telling the truth about your experience or what you are having a hard time with in the relationship. As one partner speaks, the other simply tries to hear and understand. Above all, it is important to avoid trying to assign blame.

Since it is nearly impossible to get at the real issues in the heat of a conflict, you might set aside a formal time to do this, after the fight has cooled down a bit. If you are dealing with an especially difficult issue, it helps to begin by stating your intentions in talking with each other. You might each affirm your intent to hear what your partner has to say—even though it might be painful—for the good of the relationship. Or you might agree that if you become caught up in an emotional reaction while listening, you will not indulge in it or give it your primary allegiance. Instead, your aim will be to stay present and to speak and listen with an open mind.

When speaking, it is important to tune into the truth of your own experience and talk mostly about that. If you start to characterize your partner in a negative way, he or she will become defensive and find it hard to hear what you have to say. Then you run the risk of reigniting the Argument—whose main theme is *Who's Doing What to Whom*.

When listening to what your partner is struggling with, you don't have to fix it or make it better. You also don't have to agree with it. Simply see if you can hear and understand your partner's inner experience: "Oh, *that's* what's true for you, *that's* what this brings up for you, *that's* how you see and feel this." (If you find that you *can't* hear or understand, then you could acknowledge that, and inquire into it—maybe you need to speak your own truth before you can really hear your partner's side.)

SYLVIA AND DAN

Do you want to start by affirming your intentions in creating a listening space together here?

SYLVIA (to Dan): *I want to be able to state my concerns and hear yours as well, for the good of our relationship.*

DAN (to Sylvia): *I want to get to the bottom of things so we don't keep feeling hurt or divided by the problems between us.*

Good. What is the issue you'd like to explore?

SYLVIA: *There is something we have argued about the whole first year of living together without ever resolving: I feel like I'm the only one who remembers to take care of the daily household responsibilities. If I don't remind Dan, it always falls in my lap. I can't trust him to be responsible.*

And how is that for you?

SYLVIA: *I feel sort of lost and abandoned, like Dan is not there and I've been left to deal with things all by myself. And I can't seem to contact him, which makes me feel all alone.*

Good. You're revealing your inner experience. You feel alone, and—

SYLVIA: *And lost, without any contact. I feel like I'm swimming by myself.*

Let's give Dan a chance to respond to that. It would

be helpful to do this in a formal way at first, by telling Sylvia what you heard her say, so that you don't just react automatically.

DAN (to Sylvia): *What I hear you saying is that when you have to remind me to do daily chores or mundane things, you feel really alone; you feel like I'm not there anymore, I'm not present.*

How does it affect you to hear how this is for her?

DAN: *It really makes me sad that you feel so alone and lost when I don't help out or when you have to remind me to do something. Even though we've talked about this a lot, I never knew you felt abandoned. Realizing that almost makes me want to cry.*

I noticed something happening in your face, Sylvia, when he said that. Do you want to respond to what Dan just said to you?

SYLVIA: *I felt like I just dropped down into myself. It felt like such a relief, a real relief and connection.*

Good. Could you now tell Sylvia about your side of this issue, Dan?

DAN (to Sylvia): *The way you remind me to do things feels too controlling. It would be easier to take care of these things if you didn't always ask me in such a controlling way.*

Instead of focusing on what she's doing wrong, see if you can tell her how it is for you when you feel controlled. What is that like on the inside for you?

DAN (to Sylvia): *It feels frustrating. I just want to shake you and say, "Just wait a minute! Just hold on!"*

Now you're focusing on her again. Where's that frustration coming from inside you?

DAN: *I'm not sure, but I somehow feel like a child.*

Can you say more about what's that's like for you?

DAN: *It's like I want to be able to play more; I want to be on my own schedule and not be called in from playing. I can't really articulate it any better than that.*

You're getting there. Can you say back what you hear him saying, Sylvia?

SYLVIA: *It sounds like you feel like a child who wants to play, but when I want you to do some work around the house, I become like your parent.*

DAN: *Yes, and I'm afraid that something will shut down and I won't be able to play anymore.*

What's hard about that for you?

DAN: *It's like I'm not in control, I can't do what I want.*

It sounds like you feel disempowered when she asks you to take care of the household chores.

DAN: *Yes. And then I want to resist her even more.*

Right. Because disempowerment is a serious issue. Washing the dishes, that's not a big deal, but disempowerment is.

DAN: *Feeling like a child who's being told what to do and having no choice—that's a big issue for me.*

As usual, what the problem first seems to be is not the real problem. You fight about the chores, but it doesn't go anywhere because that's not the real issue.

(To Sylvia) You started telling the truth when you shifted from telling Dan, "You're irresponsible," to admitting, "I feel at a loss and alone and abandoned in this situation."

(To Dan) You started telling the truth when you shifted from telling Sylvia, "You're too controlling," to admitting, "I feel like a disempowered child."

(To Sylvia) What's it like to have Dan let you in on how this is for him? How does that affect you?

SYLVIA: *Well, I really felt what you were saying, Dan. As you were speaking, I was thinking, "Yeah, disempowered. That's right. That's what I feel too." That's another word that would fit for me, along with lost and abandoned. So that helps me understand you a lot. We've gotten close to this before, but I never understood it that way until just now.*

DAN: *Neither had I.*

When you argue—"You don't do the dishes," or "Stop telling me what to do"—you're just butting heads. But now you have a common ground from which to talk about this, instead of polarizing into antagonistic positions. As is often the case, underneath the Argument, where you polarize into opposite positions, you both have similar feelings: You each feel lost and disempowered.

No doubt fighting is a way in which you each try to stand your ground with the other and have your own truth. But since you usually focus on what your partner is doing, instead of clarifying what's true for *you*, the fight doesn't accomplish anything.

Let's see what needs to happen in the place where you feel disempowered, so you could take another step here. You might start by contacting the raw edge of feeling powerless or abandoned, and see what you need there.

SYLVIA: *What would be helpful for me would be to develop some structure or schedule for doing the work we need to do, so that we don't keep creating this friction.*

DAN: *That's probably a good idea, so that we don't always get into our stuff around it.*

SYLVIA: *I also would like you to be sensitive to how this is for me.*

You want him to know how much it matters to you.

SYLVIA: *Exactly. I need you to know that this really matters to me.*

DAN: *I hear that. And the same for me: If we both developed the schedule together, then I wouldn't feel like I was having to give in to your pressure. I also realize that I need to be more aware of this disempowered child part of me, instead of stuffing it away somewhere. And I want you to know that when I react to doing chores, it's because of this stuff that comes up for me, not because I don't care about you.*

SYLVIA: *It's important for me to hear that.*

Here we see that even a mundane argument about household chores contains deeper issues that two people can benefit from airing. In this case, Sylvia's reaction to Dan contained a bad Other projection: She saw him as abandoning her. Dan also saw her as the bad Other, the controlling parent who wouldn't let him be free and play. And underneath their struggle, their experience is similar: They feel threatened and disempowered, and they each want to maintain their own integrity.

Through understanding what is going on for them, and communicating about that, they bring greater consciousness and empathy to this problem. And that will reduce the issue's emotional charge, which comes from the subconscious setups that their Argument activates.

GEORGE AND KATE

GEORGE: *Kate and I are having a real problem right now. One of my sons has had a financial setback and I want to help him with a loan. I made that decision unilaterally because I didn't want Kate to disagree with what I wanted to do. I didn't want her reacting to my feelings about my kid, and I didn't want her disapproval. When she found out about the loan, we had a big fight, and it's still pretty raw between us.*

How do you feel about this right now?

GEORGE: *I feel really stuck, frustrated, angry—all mixed together. I feel like I'm sinking and wanting to be rescued.*

You're bogged down, and you want to get out of it.

GEORGE: *I want to get out of it quick.*

Right. But first let's see what it's like just to be where you are.

GEORGE: *Stay in my bog, right?*

Maybe there are flowers there—swamp flowers. Would you be willing to open to the feeling of being in this bog? How are you there?

GEORGE: *I'm sad. I'm a thinker, but I can't even think here. It's a bad feeling.*

See if you can keep opening your awareness to how you're feeling. Let yourself feel the real texture and quality of this experience, without judging or reacting to it with your mind. Don't try to minimize the sadness, but give it as much room as it needs, and stay present in the middle of it.

(Long pause)

GEORGE: *As it got worse, it got better. It felt like I was there with it.*

Good. You made contact with yourself in that place.

(To Kate) What's happening for you?

KATE: *When George first started to talk, I felt constricted, as though my body were too small to hold my feelings.*

What are you feeling now?

KATE: *There's this huge, heavy feeling. I feel really sad and small and powerless and scared. And I feel all alone.*

You each have a lot of feeling, but you're both isolated in your separate capsules. Is that a familiar experience?

GEORGE: *Yes. I still want to be alone with these feelings. I don't want to share them with Kate.*

So there's one pool of feeling over here, and another pool of feeling over there. How do these two pools of feeling want to relate to each other right now? Maybe they want to stay separate, maybe not.

KATE: *I want to run away and be by myself.*

Can you tell George about that?

KATE (to George): *When we argue, I don't feel safe. I want to run away somewhere where I can be safe.*

(To George) What's it like for you to hear that?

GEORGE (to Kate): *I can hear how you feel, but I'm still cocooning, needing to protect myself.*

Yes, you're in your cocoon, but you're also acknowledging where you are, as well as making some contact right now by telling her about that. Can you tell Kate anything more about how that is for you?

GEORGE: *I still feel separated. There's a place that says, "I need to protect myself from you."*

What's it like to acknowledge that to Kate?

GEORGE: *It feels good because it's honest, it's real. I love you and I'm still scared and feeling separate.*

KATE: *It's scary for me to acknowledge to you that I want to be separate too. There's this part of me that doesn't want you to know that.*

(To Kate) Can you tell George what's going on for you when you want to be separate? Where's that coming from? Experience it inside first.

KATE: *I want to be able to control what happens to me. And I feel that if I can be separate, you can't hurt me, because then I'm in control.*

Can you feel how both sides are present for each of you right now—wanting to stay separate *and* starting to make contact? These two pools of feeling are both saying the same thing: "I'm afraid that if I really open to you, I'll be hurt." What's it like to acknowledge that with each other?

GEORGE: *We're both jerks—we want the same thing for ourselves and for each other, but we cover that up with so much fighting and screwed-up stuff that . . .*

What's it like right now *not* to cover it up? "Here it is: our fear of being hurt. We both have this." After acknowledging that, see if there's anything you want to say to each other.

GEORGE: *I want us to be able to stay here. It feels good.*

What's the "here" that feels good?

GEORGE: *Being real.*

So it's not that you've overcome your fear, but that you're acknowledging the truth of what is happening for you: "I'm afraid of opening up to you because I might get hurt."

GEORGE: *Got it.*

KATE: *It dawns on me that when we get in these separate spaces, I usually feel like I'm the little kid and you've got it all together. But when you acknowledge that you also want to stay separate because you're afraid of being hurt, that really helps me. I don't feel so alone.*

When George lets you see what's going on for him, you don't see him as the big bad Other anymore. That helps free you from your identity as the helpless child.

GEORGE: *That's how I feel too—like a little kid.*

KATE: *I can really hear that when you say it in that open kind of way. And I feel closer to you.*

(They hug.)

The problem with the loan still isn't solved, but from where you are right now, how does it look?

GEORGE: *It looks different. It doesn't feel like such a big deal.*

That issue touched a sore point in each of you. In discovering how it affects you and sharing that with each other, you start to create a ground of mutual understanding and empathy. And from there you can approach the issue of the loan in a nonoppositional way. You will still have to work out your differences, but now you can do that in a new spirit. You've created a context in which a solution can arise; seeing your partner as the bad Other is a context in which no solution is possible.

KATE: *Instead of just focusing on my fear that I won't get what I want in this situation, I feel more willing to look at what George is dealing with here.*

The most important word you just used was *willing.* When you each speak your truth and connect on a deeper level, this generates a willingness to work out your problems together. How you handle problems with George's kids will probably require some negotiated settlements. The question is: Are both parties willing to enter negotiations in good faith? It's like two warring countries: If they're not willing to find a solution, they can talk for ten years at the bargaining table without ever getting anywhere.

When two people see through their bad-Other projections—the oppositional mindset that says, "I'm hurting and you're the one who's inflicting the hurt"—and acknowledge their pain to each other, they see that they're both hurting, and they're both in this together. Then they're more than halfway toward a solution to any problem they may be facing.

MARY AND STEPHAN

What issue would you like to talk about?

MARY: *I don't feel free to speak with Stephan from my heart. It often seems that he doesn't really see or hear me when I try to share myself with him.*

(To Stephan) What's your side of this?

STEPHAN: *I feel criticized. I often hear Mary focusing on what I'm not doing right, and then I get really angry.*

(To Mary) You feel like you can't speak from your heart with Stephan.

(To Stephan) And you feel blamed and criticized about that.

What we can work on here is helping both of you to say and hear what's going on within you, underneath the conflict between you. See if you can tune in to how this situation affects you on the inside. What does it touch that feels difficult? See if you can describe your inner experience of the difficulty. Maybe Mary could start.

(To Stephan) And you could just try to hear and understand what's going on for her.

MARY: *Well, the first thing I'm aware of is a flutteriness in my belly as I start to talk about this. My nature is basically curious and outgoing. I ask a lot of questions, and that is very innocent and joyful for me. But when I was a child, nothing I said was heard or accepted by my parents. This situation with Stephan reminds me of that.*

How does it affect you when you don't feel heard?

MARY: *It makes me feel small and worthless, as though whatever I try to express has no meaning or importance. It makes me sad.*

Are you in touch with that sadness now?

MARY: *Yes.*

Can you tell Stephan about it?

MARY (to Stephan): *When I'm expressing myself to you and you become defensive, I feel very small. I don't know if I matter to you. And that makes me very sad.*

(To Stephan) Can you say back the essence of what you hear Mary saying?

STEPHAN: *When I'm not listening to you, you go to a place where you feel really small and unloved. And you get scared.*

(To Mary) Do you feel that he hears and understands you?

MARY (to Stephan): *I think that you're hearing me; I don't know if you understand.*

How does he not understand you? Maybe you need to say something more.

MARY: *I don't know. Nothing comes to me.*

Could it be that you have a hard time trusting that you're really seen and understood? Does that sound right?

MARY: *Yes.*

So instead of projecting that on Stephan, you might acknowledge that it's hard to trust that you're being seen and heard, and say what that's like for you.

MARY: *It's often hard for me to believe that I'm loved or understood. And that's very painful for me.*

STEPHAN: *I can feel how that's true for you.*

(To Mary) Do you feel that he's hearing and understanding you now?

MARY: *I do.*

Could you take a moment and let that in? You're really letting him into a very vulnerable place here.

MARY: *Mmm——hm.*

(To Stephan) Let's hear your side now. What goes on for you in this?

STEPHAN (to Mary): *When you say you don't feel heard, I start feeling that I'm bad, or not good enough, and that it's my job to fix your hurt, and I'm being blamed for not listening enough, not caring enough.*

How does it affect you when you're in that not-good-enough place?

STEPHAN: *It's hard to sense that right now.*

What's going on?

STEPHAN: *I'm experiencing fear right here.*

Could you say something about that to Mary?

STEPHAN: *When I feel blamed by you for not being there, it's like a brick in my stomach. It's like I'm stuck, with no place to go——I can't open to myself and I can't open to you. And I just end up wanting to attack you or run away.*

Let's go back to the fear. I don't think the fear by itself is the brick in your stomach. Something else is creating that brick, some kind of contraction or reaction. Let's see what that is.

STEPHAN: *It feels like something really vulnerable, like a raw wound. I have this image of an earthworm that is touched and then pulls away.*

There's a rawness, and then a pulling away from that. What's the need to pull away?

STEPHAN: *I feel so terrible about myself. It gets excruciating.*

So there's not just fear and rawness there. A judgment also comes up about yourself.

STEPHAN: *I should be able to . . .*

Right. "I should be able to . . . I should be able to do something so I don't have to feel this way." Is that it?

STEPHAN: *It's hard to sit with the rawness that comes up when Mary and I talk about this issue.*

It's hard to feel the rawness and be in contact with Mary.

STEPHAN: *Be in contact with myself.*

Yes. It's hard for you to stay in contact with yourself when it seems like Mary's not getting what she wants from you.

STEPHAN: *Yes.*

Because you blame yourself.

STEPHAN: *That's something I do most of the time.*

I'm sure you've told her that *she* blames you too much. But what would it be like to tell her about how you blame yourself?

STEPHAN (to Mary): *When you're in pain, it's hard for me not to blame myself. I always do that. And I end up hating myself. There's a lot of sadness around that for me.*

Can you allow that sadness now, stay with it?

STEPHAN: *I can't stand it. And it's happening all the time. I feel scared most of the time. . . .*

Right now I feel a tremendous amount of heat in my chest. I long for this, and it terrifies me.

What is it you long for?

STEPHAN: *This heat, this energy in my heart.*

What's it like right now to feel this energy in your heart, which arises when you open and reveal yourself?

STEPHAN: *It's sweet.*

Yes, sweet.

STEPHAN: *I touch it and then I run; I touch it and run.*

Yes.

STEPHAN: *But that's okay.*

Right, that's okay. That's what we all do. There's no need to judge that.

STEPHAN: *I see you touch it all the time, Mary, but I can't even get close to it.*

MARY: *I run, too. I usually don't stay there either.*

(To Stephan) You *are* staying there right now, that's the main thing. It's important to let yourself feel that, because it's new for you: You're very present; you're acknowledging what's going on; you're here with your heart open, even though it feels shaky and you have judgments about it. You're here with all of this right now. Let yourself feel what it's like to be here like this, while letting Mary in on it too.

STEPHAN: *I long for this and it terrifies me.*

MARY: *I understand how that feels.*

STEPHAN: *Can you see how it terrifies me?*

MARY: *Mmm——hm.*

(To Mary) Could you tell him what you understand about what he's going through?

MARY: *I hear that you blame yourself because you can't fix my pain. And that you're terrified when you go into that heart space. I really hear that and I understand it.*

And did you hear his longing for it, too?

MARY: *Yes, I did hear that. Yes, it was wonderful to hear that you felt that sweetness.*

(To Stephan) Do you feel that she understands what is going on for you in this place?

STEPHAN: *Yes.*

So just for a moment see what it's like to meet in this nakedness, with nothing to do but just be here with each other.

MARY: *Well, for me it feels scary . . . and sweet . . . and joyous . . . and there's a part that wants to pull back. All of that.*

(To Stephan) How does it feel for you?

STEPHAN: *I feel contractions coming in waves. I get a glimpse of opening and then I run; I get a glimpse and I run.*

Yes. And what you're doing right now is telling the truth about that, rather than acting out the running. You're telling the truth about your impulse to run. That's a profound step.

STEPHAN: *And I don't have to poison it by saying I'm not doing good enough.*

That's right. You can even acknowledge, in a compassionate way, how often you ask yourself, "Am I doing it good enough?"

STEPHAN: *And how I use her pain to measure that.*

Yes. That self-judgment was creating the brick in your belly.

Here we see again how quickly the Argument dissolves when two people dive beneath their blame, connect with their inner experience, and reveal that to each other. Mary's blame was, "You're not hearing and seeing me." But her deeper truth is, "It's hard for me to trust that I will be heard or seen." That's a very different statement. And Stephan's blame was, "You make me feel bad when I'm not there enough for you." But his deeper vulnerability is, "I make myself bad when I think I'm not enough for you." That switch—from projection to truth-telling—is what is essential for putting an end to the Argument.

Chapter Ten

THE INNER MARRIAGE

All life is pulsation, continually moving in waves between opposite poles: rising and falling, intensifying and releasing, coming into form and dissolving into space. The sun's life-giving energy is born of the interplay of centrifugal and centripetal forces. Similarly, our heart keeps us alive through a cyclical flow of drawing blood in and pumping it out again. In every aspect of creation, the pulse of life alternately contracts and expands, *gathering in* and *radiating out*.

These two poles of life are present in both sexes as the feminine and masculine principles. *Masculine* and *feminine* are much broader terms than *male* and *female*, which refer to the two genders. The masculine pole—which the Chinese call *yang*—is the principle of centrifugal force, expansion, separation, individuation. The feminine or *yin* principle manifests as centripetal energy, in-gathering, grounding, cohesion, and relatedness.

In the ancient Chinese view of the genders, men generally contain a larger proportion of masculine, or yang energy, while women generally contain a larger proportion of yin. An early Chinese medical text spells out the basic principle: "As a male, man belongs to yang; as a female, woman belongs to yin. Yet both, male and female, are products of two primary elements, hence both qualities are contained in both sexes."

Since the masculine and feminine energies are equal and essential halves of life, every person needs to embody and integrate both in order to be fully human. Many sacred traditions regard this inner marriage as one of life's greatest accomplishments.

On the outer level, marriage is a conventional arrangement for regulating social and sexual relations. Yet on an inner level, marriage can be seen as an alliance of two souls helping one another evolve, and as a catalyst for the integration of masculine and feminine within each of them. In this sense, the outer form of marriage becomes the symbol of an inner alchemy, as well as the crucible in which this alchemy takes place. While a marriage ceremony requires but a few minutes, the alliance between two souls takes years to ripen and develop. And beyond that, the integration of masculine and feminine within each individual can take a whole lifetime.

Two lovers' responses to each other provide a tremendous amount of information, inspiration, and guidance that can help each of them work on this inner marriage. What I am most attracted to in my partner, for instance, are those positive feminine qualities that are dormant or recessive in myself. But if I simply let her carry these qualities for me, my own inner feminine will not evolve, and no inner marriage will be possible. If instead I let my attraction to her reveal these qualities in myself, then our connection becomes my teacher, helping me find lost or forgotten regions of my soul. The golden-haired princess is inside me, and it is up to me to awaken her myself.

Conversely, what I most struggle with in my partner often points to some negative, distorted picture of the feminine that I hold in my own psyche. This negative image blocks my access to the positive feminine in myself. Therefore I can also learn to use my resistances to my partner as a teacher—to show me the obstacles to the marriage of the two halves of life inside me.

In this way, both the dance and the war of the sexes provide important information about our state of inner integration. They show us what we need to cultivate and work on in order to overcome our inner divisions and draw strength from both sides of life moving within us.

The Essence of Feminine and Masculine

To work on this inner marriage, we need to consider the nature of masculine and feminine more deeply, and see how their fruitful union becomes disrupted in the course of our development.

Our feminine or yin nature is basic ground: It is the water of life, the in-breath, the egg in the womb, the source of nourishment. The Tibetan traditions see the vastness of open space as the cosmic Mother. Out of the womb of space all things issue forth. That issuing forth is the masculine principle. Just as the heart's contraction sends blood out through our arteries, the feminine in-gathering and collectedness gives birth to outer action. Unless we are open to the nourishment of the feminine, we have little of substance to give forth.

We touch this feminine ground whenever we open to life or let ourselves be, without goal or purpose. Whenever we allow life to move freely through us, we taste the sweetness of our yin nature. We experience a certain inner glow or softening, which can feel quite passionate, even delicious, voluptuous. This kind of opening is essential for receiving any great idea, powerful insight, or spiritual transmission. When Moses stood in relation to God and received the commandments on Mount Sinai, he was in the receptive, yin position.

Having surrendered to God, Moses could then bring down the commandments, radiate his wisdom, and lead his people—which is the archetypal yang power. He had spiritual force to radiate only because he had first surrendered himself to receiving it. Artists also proceed in this way, first receiving impressions or ideas that incubate within before issuing forth as new work. The feminine is an open, receptive, nourishing presence, while the masculine is a radiating, expanding, penetrating presence.

Two Sides of Genuine Power

Real power and creativity arise out of the union of masculine and feminine, which are like two streams converging to form a much larger flow of energy. Our primary access to this power comes through our yin openness and receptivity, as D. H. Lawrence points out:

> If a man or a woman or a race or a nation is to be anything at all, he must have the generosity to admit that his strength comes to him from beyond. It is not his own, self-generated. It comes as electricity comes, out of nowhere. . . . To live, life must come to us . . . and we must not try to get a stranglehold upon it. From beyond comes to us the power of life, the power to live, and we must wisely keep our hearts open.

In describing how real power comes to us from beyond the personality, and how we must open our hearts if we are to receive this power, Lawrence is speaking of the feminine side of our nature. Next he speaks of the masculine: "But the life will not come *unless* we live." We receive new life only if we radiate or give forth what we have received.

"That settles two points," Lawrence continues, providing the most beautiful definition of power I have come across: "First, *power is life rushing into us.*" Here he emphasizes the primacy of the feminine aspect of power, the receptive. "Second, the exercise of power is the setting of life in motion. Power is *pouvoir*: to be able to. Might: the ability to make, to bring about that which may be." Having received life, we must give life, set life in motion, set about actualizing our seed potentials. This is the masculine aspect of power.

Lawrence continues: "But in an age that, like ours, has lost the mystery of power, and the reverence for power, a false power is substituted." *The mystery of power*—how strange this phrase sounds in a culture where authority seems to belong to those who use money, technology, or weaponry to dominate and exploit. True power is a mystery because "it is given to us, from the beyond." Unfortunately, our culture has little understanding of the yin half of power—how genuine authority can only spring from opening and surrendering to life.

False power—domination—is spurious because it does not enhance life. It springs from the ego-based mentality of "I am the master of my fate, the captain of my soul"—which puts a stranglehold on life by trying to control it. When yang power manifests in this way, it becomes toxic, spawning pollution and devastation.

Lawrence suggests a simple way to distinguish between these two types of power: "*True power*, as distinct from this spurious power, *never belongs to us*" (my italics). Recognizing the sacredness of this larger force, Lawrence concludes with a benediction: "Blessed are the powerful, for theirs is the kingdom of earth."

This "kingdom of earth," born of the marriage of masculine and feminine, is a grounded power whose source is our ability to receive life and whose expression is our ability to give life. The two halves of our nature meet and join in the heart, that open gateway where we are most easily penetrated and where we also have the most to give.

Distorted Imprints

In an ideal world our parents or the elders of the community would manifest and integrate these two dimensions of power, and transmit their essence to us. Our mother or the female elders would embody the cosmic feminine principle, along with whatever yang capacities they also possessed. They would model the supportive, spacious, nourishing qualities that provide a child with the ability to trust and receive. Our father or the male elders would embody and express the radiant masculine, along with having access to yin receptivity. Their most important transmission would be to provide guidance and vision, based on an understanding of the larger purpose of human life. This gives children a framework of values and a sense of protection, helping them relate to the world with confidence and curiosity. A healthy society would also appreciate and celebrate the interplay between men and women, as a model of how the two halves of life serve each other and work together for the common good.

In societies organized around tribes or extended families, children are often exposed to a wide variety of adults who can model these qualities for them, even if their parents do not. However, those of us growing up in isolated nuclear families inevitably internalize the lopsided ways in which our parents express the masculine and feminine principles. Our other models come mostly from television and movies, which rarely portray well-integrated men and women, or their interaction.

If our mother is cold, manipulative, or engulfing, we are likely to develop a distorted image of the feminine—which will make it hard for us to trust, let go, and receive love and nourishment in our relationships. Similarly, if our father is remote, abusive, or lacking in spiritual radiance or vision, we will, like so many people today, harbor a deep suspicion of masculine assertiveness and drive. We may also have difficulty feeling inner strength and confidence, or acting boldly and decisively.

These distorted images of the masculine and feminine will also restrict our capacity for mutuality in intimate relationships. Lacking trust, we will have difficulty letting down our defenses and letting love in. Lacking confidence, we will have difficulty standing our ground and giving ourselves freely and abundantly.

Even if we have partial access to the genuine masculine and feminine, it may still be difficult to bring these two sides together if we have grown up lacking evidence of their dynamic, fruitful union. When yin and yang are divorced within us, each takes on a distorted form and we become caricatures: the helpless female and the toxic, overbearing male, the devouring mother and the remote father, the nagging wife and the wimpy husband. Our whole culture suffers from these distortions. Because we have few models of healthy, vital marriages, few people grow up with a clear sense of the positive synergy between masculine and feminine.

And because the feminine has been debased for thousands of years, this side of our nature has been damaged in everyone—men and women alike. Women who have felt mistreated by men or devalued by our culture may have difficulty trusting and allowing their softness, and this cuts them off from their yin power. Men who fear and armor themselves against the feminine also have difficulty expressing life-affirming yang strength. They dominate instead of radiate.

Working with the Inner Male and Female

Even if we have witnessed few models of the positive masculine or feminine while growing up, we can still discover these powers within us, for they are cosmic energies, as well as aspects of our essential nature. First, however, we must dislodge the negative imprints from the past that are obscuring them. Intimate relationship can help with this, because two people's interaction always reflects and reveals exactly where the inner masculine and feminine are either blocked or flowing freely.

As a way into this inquiry, it can be helpful to personify these two energies as an inner male and female. Let's say that I feel outraged when my partner fails to treat me in an all-loving, nurturing way. If I take this as a reflection of what is going on inside me, it shows me that I am cut off from my own nurturing, abundant feminine side. Then I can look at what is happening with this part of myself. Is my inner female wounded or constrained in some way? How does my inner male relate to her? Does he welcome her or reject her? Does he join with her or cut himself off from her? Is she afraid of him or does she feel unappreciated? What do these two parts of myself need to work out before they can join together in a creative alliance? Maybe they need to engage in a dialogue, get to know each other better, and work out their mutual distrust or resentment.

Of course, personifying inner male and female figures inside us is metaphoric. This kind of imagining acts on us like a fairy tale, which can reveal parts of our psyche and affect us deeply even though we know it is make-believe. So we can be imaginative, rather than literal-minded, in using this method. That will also help us discover not just a single inner male or female, but rather a whole pantheon of masculine and feminine energies at work in us.

Lisa was a creative and intelligent woman, but she had a hard time focusing her energies and bringing projects to completion. Her husband, by contrast, was a highly accomplished workaholic. Though she would criticize him for not being able to relax and enjoy himself, she secretly envied his ability to get things done. And though he would accuse her of not taking life seriously enough, he secretly envied her ability to let go and relax. The way they polarized in this regard portrayed a similar division they each experienced within themselves.

To help Lisa work with her difficulty in focusing, I asked her to consider whether the polarization with her husband reflected some division within herself. She saw an image of a hard-driving male and a collapsed female within her. The aggressive male was cast in the image of her father, who had been a highly successful overachiever and perfectionist; while the helpless female was like her mother, who had spent much of her life sunk in a state of denial and apathy.

Whenever Lisa tried to accomplish some project, the overbearing male in her psyche would push her to perform according to impossibly high standards. Meanwhile, her inner female, feeling manipulated and degraded by these harsh demands, would rebel by engaging in a sit-down strike. This inner discord reflected how her father and mother had interacted when she was young. And her inner paralysis reflected the very impasse her parents had come to in their marriage.

This realization helped Lisa liberate her genuine masculine and feminine qualities from these old childhood imprints. Behind the pushiness of the hard-driving male, she discovered *determination*—to pursue her deepest truth and realize her deepest potential. But she saw that it was impossible to realize these aims by running roughshod over her feminine side. Her inner male would have to learn to become more considerate, more gallant, by honoring the needs, rhythms, and sensitivities of her inner female. As this inner tyranny subsided, Lisa's feminine wisdom was able to come forth, showing her how she could work, while still remaining relaxed. Her inner female had much to teach the inner male about how to be—how to live in the body, bring the senses alive, and act from there.

Lisa's husband had a similar inner dynamic, except that his male side was able to steamroller his inner female and force his will upon her. However, he often suffered the

consequences in the form of bodily ailments—hyperten-
sion, stress, and fatigue. His tension and Lisa's listlessness
were both symptoms of souls divided against themselves.

As Lisa recovered her authentic masculine drive, she
experienced a new sense of initiative that provided inner
direction and purpose. And as she uncovered her feminine
wisdom, she experienced a new kind of inner support for
her work, and a deeper sense of peace.

Wisdom and Skillful Means

The feminine and masculine energies within us are always
seeking to rouse each other so that they can join together in
a mutually empowering communion. Western mysticism
describes this sacred marriage as the union of Sophia
(wisdom) and Logos (the active force of intelligence), while
Buddhism sees it as the union of wisdom and compassion.
Wisdom is regarded as feminine—not just in the Orient, but
also in the Bible and in Greek philosophy—because it arises
out of openness, and an open mind and heart are the source
of true understanding. And compassion is regarded as masculine because it is the active expression of wisdom—as
skillful means. Skillful activity involves responding appropriately to what different situations call for—destroying what
needs to be destroyed and caring for what needs our care—
for the greater good of all. The king who is benevolent, just,
and devoted to the welfare of his people symbolizes the
radiant masculine, the consort of the queen of wisdom.

Tibetan art portrays the union of wisdom and skillful
means erotically as male and female deities making love,
usually surrounded by a radiant fiery halo. With eyes wide
open and arms waving, the two lovers smile fiercely. They
are obviously waking each other up! Their blissful play
tells us that this sacred union is the crown of human
development and the birthplace of enlightened action.

DIALOGUE 10A

Relationship as an Outer Mirror
of the Inner Marriage

How we respond to the one we love can provide useful
information about the state of integration between the
masculine and feminine within us. What most attracts us
in our partner often points to some quality we need to
cultivate more fully, and what bothers us most often
points to some negative imprint that interferes with inner
integration.

To explore this experientially, consider what you find
most appealing in your partner or in the opposite sex in
general, what most attracts you or turns you on. Now use
this quality as a mirror: If you're a woman, regard it as an
aspect of the positive masculine within you; if you're a
man, regard it as an aspect of your positive inner feminine.
Then personify it: What does this inner male or female
look like? What are his or her qualities? What is it like to
acknowledge him or her? What does he or she need in
order to develop more fully?

You can do the same with the quality that bothers you
most in your partner or in the opposite sex generally.
If you're a man, this may reflect some aspect of your own
distorted or atrophied inner feminine, and vice versa for
women. What does your negative inner female or male
look like? How does he or she create inner discord or block
integration within you?

Finally, you might consider what needs to happen
between the two sides before they can work together as
allies within you.

SHEILA

I really surprised myself. What I found myself valuing most in my husband was his practicality.

What do you mean by practicality?

I mean an action-oriented, goal-directed quality. My appreciation of that surprised me because we have a running quarrel about it: I usually complain that he is too practical. I say, "You're so caught up in doing that you don't value just being. I want to spend more intimate time with you in ways that are not goal directed."

And yet—and I got tears in my eyes when I realized this—I am actually drawn to my partner because of his mastery of things, even though I do nothing but criticize him for it. I remember the time I came back from being in China for three years and felt overwhelmed because I wasn't able to deal with New York City. He was masterful at it, and that made me feel great.

So there's something here to look at. Let's call this action-oriented quality an aspect of your inner male. Usually you dislike it, or it seems alien to you. What would it be like to acknowledge this as part of yourself?

I'm afraid it would make me unfeeling or callous.

Is that how you see your husband when he's being practical?

Yes, I often do.

That's because you see this masculine quality in a negative light. You seem to regard "doing" as antifeminine, unfeeling, hard-edged. So there's a split inside you—you're attracted to this aspect of yourself, but you also have negative judgments about it.

It's easier to see the hard time I have with this in my husband than in myself. We went to Italy for our honeymoon, and when we came back he acted as though, "Okay, the honeymoon's over—it's time to get back to reality," but I wasn't ready. We must be on the fiftieth installment of this Argument by now. It taps into something really deep. It makes me crazed.

What exactly makes you so crazed? If we can see where that feeling is coming from, it will reveal the negative imprint.

I'm from a working-class family in which work came first and was always valued above everything else. Everyone had to work so hard that there was no time for feelings; the whole personal side of our life was sacrificed to the work ethic. Even being in school wasn't valued. When I got scholarships to go to college, I felt as though I were betraying the family ethic. It's been hard to feel proud of my accomplishments because they don't qualify as real work in my family's eyes. This has been very painful for me.

So—"Be practical! Get down to business! No nonsense!"—you must really hate that.

Yes, passionately.

Of course there's nothing wrong with working hard or being practical. But your family expressed an extreme, distorted version of this yang quality because they didn't also value the softer, subtler yin qualities of inwardness or personal reflection. Because your family overvalued work and devalued your feminine sensitivities, you internalized that imbalance. And that created negative imprints in you. Personifying this, we might say that your inner female has been wounded by an overemphasis on the yang; and your inner male has been wounded by being cut off from the yin.

Yes, I can feel both sides of that.

What is it about your husband's action-stance that bothers you the most?

It seems driven to me. I accuse him of being a workaholic.

Is there a driven part of you?

That sounds like my shadow. I don't like to admit it, but I get all tense and stressed-out when I have a lot to do.

It sounds like your doing is cut off from your being. The inner male becomes tense and agitated because he works in a way that is cut off from the feminine.

That's right.

If you could imagine healing your partner of his driven, workaholic tendency, how would you do that? What would cure him of that?

Time—unstructured time, play time. Time for just hanging out, for just being.

Now if you take that as a mirror of what *you* need inside, what do you see?

I guess I need to learn to relax into myself more. I usually imagine that I won't be able to relax like that unless I am with someone who can hang out with me and just be, in that soft, intimate way.

Yes. That is your inner male speaking right now— calling out for the feminine. He is saying that he needs to connect with the feminine in order to relax and open up.

I guess a lot of men in this culture feel that way.

That's why we often search for the playful, delicious qualities of our own nature in women.

So your reaction to your husband's practical orientation reveals what is blocking your own inner marriage: Your feminine side—the part of you that wants to hang loose, be playful, and live in the moment—is at odds with your masculine side—the part of you that accomplishes things. Because these two sides don't know how to work together, the male remains uptight and the female remains frustrated.

I must say that this is amazing to me—how I have external-ized this struggle so completely. I can't believe it.

Yes, it's amazing. We all do that.

It's a relief to see that the real struggle is not with my partner—that I am actually wanting to bring these two sides together inside myself.

But what you usually do instead is to try to change your husband.

And it doesn't work, because my efforts to make him change only make him resist me more.

It also doesn't work because you are trying to heal an internal split externally. You imagine that if only he were different, then you could relax and play.

Instead, what would it be like to recognize and honor the abundant, playful feminine in you first—the one your family so neglected? See if you can do that right now.

That feels wonderful.

What feels so wonderful?

Saying yes to this part of me—it gives me a feeling of fullness and softness at the same time. It's astounding—that gives me a whole new sense of direction.

You're seeing a path for yourself here, which is much more interesting than struggling to change your partner. So when you find yourself criticizing him for being too practical, let that remind you to look within. You could stop and ask yourself, "What am I needing to connect with in myself right now? Where is my own playfulness?"

As the bountiful, nourishing feminine comes more alive in you, she might even start calling out to your husband's playful side, and lure him away from his work. And when your masculine side connects up with the spacious, flowing quality of the feminine, then your own doing can become skillful means—potent, dynamic action.

So my struggle with my husband around this issue is a way of trying to integrate these two sides of myself.

Yes. It reflects your need to bring about an inner marriage. This is not to deny that your husband may also have a problem here that needs to be addressed. But you will be able to confront what is going on in him more clearly and skillfully if you work first with your own inner split.

RICHARD

I'm tired of always having to be the strong one in relationships. I would like to find a woman who could stand her ground, be confident, and not always rely on me to take charge.

Now take this as a mirror: In seeking this kind of woman, are you also saying, "If my inner female were stronger, then maybe I could relax"?

Yes. I always have to be responsible, on guard. I have a hard time just flowing freely with my feelings. And I would like to be able to.

Okay. Let's personify this responsible part of you as an inner male. What is he like?

He's anxious. I had to be hypervigilant as a child to avoid being attacked for the way I was. That makes it hard for me to let down and feel at ease.

What does this anxious part of you need?

To know that someone strong will be there for me. If I had a woman like that, it would be easier for me to let down.

Again, let's take what you're looking for in a woman as symbolic of what you are needing to connect with in yourself. Your inner male wants to let down the guard he's always maintaining. If the inner female were a strong presence, letting him know she was right there beside him, that support would help him relax. Then you could let down and let your feelings flow.

Right . . . But I have a difficult time with that. I imagine that I would just be in tears.

Be in tears?

Be in tears—for a long time—if I really let down and acknowledged the tragedies in my life and my sorrow about them.

What are you needing in this place of sorrow?

Someone to be with me who wasn't afraid of that.

Yes, that's what you are looking for in a woman— someone who would not be afraid if you let down, cried, and felt the sadness you're holding back. Someone who could just be there, without wavering, like the earth itself. Then you could really let down.

Yes.

Well, there's someone inside you who can do that— your own inner female. Of course, this is only metaphorical—we are really talking about a quality of your soul. But it can be helpful to personify it for a moment. Can you imagine this inner female who could be there for you, to support you and allow the anxious, hypervigilant male to settle down, feel his feelings, and be himself? How does that feel?

It's a tremendous relief.

Yes, a relief. And how else does it affect you?

It's hard to put it into words. It gives me a sense of peace and calm.

Yes. When you find that ground of support that allows you to go through whatever you need to go through, you start to calm down inside.

I can sense that, but there's also something scary about trying to do this on my own.

Well, this is a new edge for you. Here is where the notion of *path* can be helpful: Cultivating a relationship with the earthy, grounded feminine side of yourself is an ongoing process that will unfold in steps and stages. You have just taken the first step—recognizing your longing to connect with this part of you. Once you connect with a deep longing, a path naturally starts to unfold. And as you connect with that inner support, it will be less scary to face your feelings.

I know what you mean. I've had glimpses of this—when I feel this kind of inner support, my ability to trust increases, and along with that, my strength and confidence increase. They seem to work together.

That's exactly the point. When a man cultivates his feminine powers, then his masculine side also becomes more powerful. In your case, feeling inner support allows you to relax, and then you feel more confident about being yourself.

ROSE MARIE

When I did this exercise, I got in touch with my own distorted male for the first time ever. That was quite an awakening. I realized that he was uncaring and unprotective of me, like my father, who was an alcoholic. My inner female was really angry at him. She wanted him to snap out of it and start protecting her.

That quality of feminine wrath is very powerful. It says to the male, "Come on! Wake up! We need you here!"

My male side just wants to sleep. His attitude is, "Do it your-self. I can't be bothered." My female side is wounded because I haven't had many experiences of the positive male—strong, protec-tive, forward-looking, reliable. That leaves her feeling powerless and helpless.

How does she feel about that?

I'm angry about not having a positive inner male who honors my softness and helps me move forward. Instead he shames me when I feel vulnerable. Yes, that makes me angry.

Can you let yourself acknowledge and allow that anger?

It's amazing. When I really feel my anger about this, I also contact a protective, stalwart part of myself. I don't feel so helpless.

Yes. In acknowledging your anger about the absence of the genuine male, you start to feel your strength, which *is* the genuine, powerful male showing up and coming to meet you.

That is revealing and exciting at the same time. It gives me a whole new sense of what is possible.

Chapter Eleven

MEN IN RELATIONSHIP

*The thing is for men to have the courage to draw
nearer to women, expose themselves to them. . . .
When man and woman actually meet, there is
always terrible risk to both of them. We have to meet
as I meet a jaguar between the trees in the mountains,
and advance, and touch, and risk it. . . .
To be a man is to risk your body and blood first,
and then to risk your mind. All the time,
to risk your known self, and become once more a self
you could never have known or expected.*

D. H. LAWRENCE

The male spirit is always seeking new challenges, willing to risk body and mind, as Lawrence suggests, to forge a path into unexplored territory. Men today tend to define their challenges in terms of outer pursuits and conquests: exploring creative frontiers, forging new scientific advances, crafting business and political deals, or pushing the limits of their physical endurance. Yet for all their expertise in worldly affairs, most men are still primitives in their relationships with women—because fully engaging with a woman means probing the uncharted depths of their own inner life. This is the new frontier for men today.

The Dialectic of Male Development

Men love and need to engage in heroic deeds. For thousands of years men have defined heroism in terms of separating from women and setting out on their own, like Ulysses leaving Penelope to join the Trojan War. And indeed, breaking free from dependency on mother and women in general, in order to forge a path of one's own, is an essential step in male development. A man usually discovers his deepest sense of purpose in moments of being alone with his own soul.

Yet many men stop there, never realizing that there is a larger dialectic of male development, beyond just establishing a separate identity apart from women. Maleness starts out as a oneness with femaleness, quite literally: The male fetus begins its development as a female, until the male chromosome eventually takes effect, initiating the development of the male organs and eliminating the embryonic female organs that have begun to grow. Yet within the womb and for many months after birth, the male infant still remains totally bonded with his mother. Unlike girls, whose identification with their mother supports their gender development, a boy must, to establish a male identity, eventually "renounce his connection with the one who has been so deeply embedded in his psychic life as to seem a part of himself. It's a demanding, complicated, and painful process that takes its toll on a boy," as psychologist Lillian Rubin describes it. If the first stage of male development is unity with the feminine, the second stage involves separation, differentiation.

Men often remain stuck at one of these first two

stages of development: either psychically tied to their mother, or else hardened into a reactive macho stance, out of fear of being engulfed by the feminine that was once the ground of their existence. In his relations with women, a man who is stuck at the first stage will remain a child, at the second, an adolescent, and at either one, someone driven by unconscious reactivity.

The rise of interest in men's work—where men in small groups help each other move through these stages and cultivate a deeper appreciation of themselves as men—has been a positive force in recent years. Yet once a man finds his masculine ground, apart from women, another step is necessary if he wants to further his unfolding and form healthy intimate relationships. He must become receptive once more to what women can teach him. In this way he brings the dialectic full circle: from unconscious fusion with the feminine to a new, more conscious communion. This is the only way for a man to become a true adult in his relationships.

Taking this further step calls for a different brand of heroism from that of stage two, where a man breaks away from the feminine in order to find himself. Our culture as a whole is overly fascinated with the second stage of this dialectic, often portrayed purely in terms of conquest or ascent. While there is a place for ascent in male development—a young man's spirit needs to spread its wings and soar—our culture has become fixated on this kind of heroism. Our modern heroes are those who endlessly ascend—to the top of the Hit Parade or best-seller charts, to the top floors of skyscrapers where the corporate headquarters reside, into the heavens in rocket ships, or into the disembodied mental realm via computers or virtual reality. The heroism of stage three, by contrast, involves facing and overcoming some of our deepest fears—about coming down to earth, coming into our body, relating with our feelings, and committing ourselves to a path of passionate engagement with the world.

As a man negotiates this third stage, the dialectic of his development will continue to unfold. For in order to open more fully to the feminine, a man must root himself more firmly in genuine masculine power. He can no longer afford, in D. H. Lawrence's words, to "go forth panoplied in his own idea of himself," but must forge a deeper knowledge of who he is, beyond any *image* of what it is to be a man. In mythic terms, to have a queen he must become a king. Then when he spends time apart from women or in companionship with other men, this will not be a form of reacting or turning against, but a simple expression of who he is.

A Different Brand of Heroism

One of the great secrets of men—secret in the sense that we rarely admit it among ourselves—is that we are afraid of women. It takes great courage and strength for a man to meet a woman with an open heart and mind, to be receptive to what she has to teach, or to hold his own ground in the face of her emotional intensity or earthy strength. On one level, this is because our mothers were all-powerful when we were young and helpless. The son stands in a yin, receptive relation to his mother, who is yang in relation to him. Ideally the father or a group of elder males would help a young man separate from his mother and find his own yang strength. But many men today, lacking this kind of mentoring and support from older males, have had to wage their own lonely, titanic struggle to free themselves from their mother's emotional grip. Such men do not readily give in to a woman's influence again.

On another level, a man's fear of woman reflects an inner suspicion and distrust of his own yin nature, his softer, more receptive side. We are afraid that being open and yielding will undermine our power, identity, autonomy. And this fear keeps us on guard in our relations with women, especially if we believe that our strength resides only on our masculine side, and if we are unfamiliar with the larger power that springs from the integration of masculine and feminine within us.

Although intimate relationship provides one of the best vehicles for helping us forge this integration, not many men are able to make use of it in this way. We often imagine that relationship is a woman's specialty, something that belongs within her sphere of influence. And this causes us to miss, or fail to appreciate, the many opportunities it offers for our own soulwork, for deep inner reconciliation and synergy between our different powers and potentials.

In order to make use of these opportunities, men need to develop their own vision of relationship, instead of seeing this aspect of life as a woman's sphere. One way to forge such a vision is by reclaiming the original meaning of romantic love—as a sacred and heroic undertaking. Although romance today is often associated with trivial notions of hearts and flowers, this was not originally the case. The word *romance* comes from the French word for the novel, *roman*. The original *roman* was a tale of chivalry and brave deeds that the lover performed for the sake of his beloved, as an essential step in his own spiritual development.

When we speak of the romance of mountain climbing, of setting out to sea in a small boat, or of walking alone on the moors at night, we draw close to this original meaning of the word. These activities have a certain romance because they test us, call on all our resources, and bring us to an edge, where we move out of our familiar comfort zone. Romantic love poses a similar challenge because it impels a man, in Rilke's words, "to ripen, to become world, to become world for himself for another's sake; it is a great exacting claim upon him, something that chooses him out and calls him to vast things."

This is what happens when a woman's influence starts to work on us—it calls us to vast things—first of all by bringing us to an edge where we fear to tread. The kind of heroism required here calls for hand-to-hand combat with the demons of fear we encounter on the threshold of the unknown—when we approach the dark continent of the feminine, which we usually regard as alien and Other. In order to rise to this challenge, we need to re-vision relationship as a great transformative work that requires and calls forth wisdom and courage.

Woman as Activator

The traditional model of male/female relations in our society portrays man as active or dynamic and woman as passive or receptive. This one-dimensional perspective has some truth on the physical plane, where a man's body has a greater proportion of muscle tissue, and is thus more oriented toward forceful exertion. According to many sacred traditions, however, the polarities reverse when we move from the outer to the inner plane.

While the masculine is more active on the outer, physical plane, sacred tradition recognizes the feminine as more dynamic on the inner, subtle plane of vital energy and feeling. Mythical figures such as the king of the gods—Zeus in Greek religion, or Indra in Hinduism—represent man's predominance on the outer plane; while on the inner plane we find the queen of wisdom—Sophia, Isis, Inanna/Ishtar, the Shekinah—holding sway.

While muscle power generates force and movement in the outer, physical body, a deeper life force governs the inner, "subtle body" and its flows of energy. The Western esoteric traditions regard this vital force that animates the body, the living soul—*anima*—as feminine. Likewise, the Hindus know this dynamic activator as Shakti, the consort of the great Shiva, whose nature is more lunar and quiescent in relation to her.

A woman who is in touch with her shakti energy radiates heat, emanating from the transformative fire of her vital force. And she often has access to a special kind of wisdom that can guide a man on the inner plane. Since she is often more attuned than he is to the subtle energy currents flowing within, one of her greatest functions in his life is to arouse him—to stir him to feel. If a man is often a woman's teacher, protector, and guide in the visionary, intellectual, and worldly spheres, a woman often leads and inspires a man by teaching him to come into his body, rouse his vitality, listen to his heart-consciousness, and dance with life's energies.

The story of Naropa, one of the great Tantric masters of ancient India, illustrates how provocative, arousing feminine energy can help spur a man's development. Naropa at midlife was the greatest scholar at Nalanda, the most prominent Buddhist university of his day. He was a brilliant philosopher, skilled logician, and accomplished yogi—the pinnacle of success according to the standards of his time.

One day when Naropa was immersed in his books, a shadow fell over them. He looked up to see an ugly old hag, who asked him if he understood what he was reading: "In regard to the Buddha's teaching, do you understand the *words* or the *sense* (the inner meaning)?" When Naropa answered, "I understand the words," the hag laughed and danced. "I am happy, Naropa," she said, "that you speak the truth." But when Naropa went on to say, "And I also understand the sense," she began to scream and tear out her hair. Glaring fiercely at Naropa, she called him a liar.

This encounter with the hag shocked Naropa into realizing that he was not as spiritually advanced as he had thought. Although he had devoted his whole life to studying and practicing the Buddha's teachings, he had not realized their essential meaning. When he asked her how to grasp the true meaning, she sent him in search of his guru, who would eventually help him attain complete spiritual realization.

The hag in this story was a dakini who manifested to shake Naropa up and spur him to dive deeper into life. In the Tibetan tradition a dakini is a playful/wrathful sky goddess, who embodies a wild, provocative energy that enters people's lives and shakes them loose from complacency and superficiality. The dakini's nature is to rouse, inspire, and challenge people to go deeper—to face their fears and take a leap, to give up false beliefs about themselves and discover their true nature.

Most men in our culture desperately need this kind of shaking up. By the time we reach midlife, most of us have focused our energies so totally on outer accomplishments that we have become a dry, empty shell inside. A man's midlife crisis often springs from recognizing that everything he has achieved—career, success, wealth, wife, and family—feels strangely hollow and disappointing; it does not provide the sense of joy and significance his soul most longs for. And so it is at the peak of Naropa's career that the wrathful dakini appears, to rouse him out of his complacency, throw him back into beginner's mind, and awaken him to the greater mysteries.

Many women have had this kind of effect on men. In the film of William Nicholson's biographical play *Shadowlands*, Joy Gresham, an American poet, takes on this role when she enters the life of the renowned English writer C. S. Lewis. Though she appreciates Lewis's penetrating mind, gentle spirit, and soulful refinement, she can also see that his life as a fifty-four-year-old bachelor has become far too predictable and safe. Nothing in his carefully circumscribed world forces him to risk himself or his feelings.

Instead of trying to fit into his comfort zone, Joy Gresham cuts through Lewis's defenses, shakes up his frame of reference, and kindles his inner fire. In a scene reminiscent of Naropa's encounter with the hag, she turns on him in his academic quarters at Oxford and chides him: "Everyone you have contact with is younger than you, weaker than you, or under your control. You've arranged a life for yourself where no one can touch you." And with that she storms out, leaving the great Oxford don speechless and bewildered.

In their brief marriage, C. S. Lewis came to realize the immense gift his wife had given him by challenging him to come alive and be more vitally present with her. "How many bubbles of mine she pricked!" wrote Lewis after her early death, comparing her to a leopard who, when it "scented the first whiff of cant ... sprang and knocked you over before you knew what was happening." He had discovered what the Indian Tantrics had known a thousand years before: "Women are the supreme fire of transformation."

Emotional Honesty and the Sword of Discrimination

A woman often plays this role of *agent provocateur* in a man's life by asking for more than he is willing or able to give— more intimacy, more feeling, more honest communication, more expressions of warmth and connectedness. She may also see what he needs for his emotional and spiritual development more clearly than he does himself.

Yet a man may have a hard time responding when a woman challenges him to be more available or more personally expressive. This is understandable. For a man, revealing himself or exposing his feelings may take him beyond his usual area of competence or expertise. Suddenly he is asked to do something that no one even taught him to value before. Not knowing what to do, not having the answers, he feels put on the spot, anxious, instantly defensive.

Situations like this are especially confusing if we fail to recognize the fourfold truth often operating here. The woman may have a genuine concern: she wants more direct, soulful contact, she doesn't feel the man's heart fully open to her, or she needs to know if he can really be there for her. But at the same time, she may be expressing her concern in a critical or aggressive way, perhaps because she is projecting an image of her absent father onto the man. The man's truth is that he has a hard time matching her emotional intensity, his style of making contact is different from hers, or he wants her to accept him as he is. But he may also react to her concerns defensively and shut down, perhaps because he is seeing her as his demanding mother. Then, instead of responding to each other's truth, both partners become lost in reacting to each other's distortions.

To work with this kind of situation, it helps to see how the reversed polarity discussed earlier is operating here: While men may be more forceful on the outer plane and more quickly roused to action, women are more dynamic on the inner plane and more quickly roused to feeling. Therefore, a woman is quicker to know and say what she feels than a man, who tends to be much slower and shyer in this regard, just as he often wants to move into action sexually at a faster pace than she does, because her body responds more slowly than his.

This explains why men often feel overpowered or overwhelmed when women demand greater emotional presence. When it comes to sex, a woman often needs to be wooed, courted, slowly and gently aroused. If a man insists that she adapt to his quicker pace, she feels that he is not being caring or considerate, and this leads to conflict. The same thing happens in reverse on the emotional plane. Just as a woman has a hard time being instantly present for a man sexually, so a man finds it difficult to be instantly present for a woman emotionally.

When a woman expects a man to follow her pace in this regard, she triggers one of his greatest fears—feeling inadequate. And this causes him to recoil. As a man in one of my workshops pointed out:

Since I can't give birth, feeling adequate is often what gives me a sense of value. So when I feel inadequate, I withdraw and go into a funk. I respond in a primal way, like a woman does when her children are threatened. This is really primitive stuff.

When a man sees himself as inadequate, he feels one-down and at risk. The woman looms large and he fears that she is starting to unman him. While she becomes more and more frustrated about not being met, he grows more and more withdrawn.

It is important that both women and men recognize what is happening here, so they don't take it so personally. If a woman can understand that a man has a slower response time, and needs gentle encouragement in revealing his feelings, just as she often does in the realm of sex, this will help her avoid becoming righteously indignant and militant when this disparity arises. And if a man can also understand what is happening here, he will less likely become paralyzed with fear or shame. He can draw his sword of discrimination, distinguishing between his *feelings*—"I *feel* helpless, lost, uncertain how to proceed"—and the old *story* from childhood that they trigger—"I *am* inadequate."

Making this discrimination will help him acknowledge his truth in these situations—"I'm having a hard time here because I'm not sure what I'm feeling or how to express it, so I don't know what to say when you ask for instant emotional contact"—without imagining that it means he is weak or unmanly. This kind of honesty will bring him into a place of grounded presence, where he can be in contact with his partner, while remaining in touch with himself.

Moments like this—when a man's expertise is put into question and he's not sure what to do next—are reminiscent of Naropa's encounter with the hag. They challenge his complacency and force him to find a deeper source of power: being open and honest with his experience in the moment. In such moments a man begins to join the two sides of his nature—strength and softness—on the spot.

Often a man resists revealing his inner experience because he imagines that this would require him to adopt a female mode of expression that is not his own. In truth, however, to be present and honest with one's experience is equally challenging for both men and women, in different ways. If the common male pitfall is being too removed from feelings, the common female pitfall is being too identified with them. Neither of these fosters deep rapport.

Honest communication is possible only when two people share their real experience with one another. This requires a capacity both for being in touch with feelings—generally a woman's strength—and for detached reflection, stepping back and opening up space around the feelings—generally a man's strength. (Humor is also possible only when we can see things in this more detached, spacious way; that is why a man is often the one to inject a Hermes-like irreverence into intimate moments, when a woman is becoming too sober or serious.)

The art of intimate conversation thus involves a fine balance between emotional responsiveness (often a woman's gift) and holding these responses in a larger perspective (often a man's gift). Although men often think of communication as a woman's specialty, it is important for them to realize that their contribution is equally important here. A man and a woman must bring their different gifts together if they are to find a genuine point of connection where they can meet like "jaguars in the mountains, and advance, and touch, and risk it."

Balancing Strength and Softness

One of a man's deep fears about opening to the feminine is that he will wind up feeling disempowered, like wild man

Samson when Delilah cut off his hair. In mythical terms, Delilah seems to represent a distorted, diabolic element in some women that is hostile to men, that seeks to disempower them as a way to feel more powerful themselves. A superficial interpretation of the Samson/Delilah story is that men who let down their guard with this aggressive element in a woman risk being castrated.

But Samson's disempowerment can be understood in another way as well. At first glance it appears that he loses his strength because he has lost his hair. But the reverse is also true: He loses his hair because he has already given up his power. Though Samson is a tough and wily fighter in battle, his prowess crumbles in his relations with women. Philosopher Julius Evola describes this type of man: "The activist man busy with doing and producing, the athlete, or the man with an 'iron will' is among the most helpless of men before the more subtle power of woman." And so Samson reveals his weakness and naivete by telling Delilah his secret—that cutting his hair will debilitate him—even though she has already thrice demonstrated her intent to betray him to the Philistines.

The strength of a fighter like Samson does not penetrate much deeper than his muscles. He is hard on the outside and squishy on the inside, because he does not really know himself, because he has always covered up his raw edges with bravado. A true spiritual warrior, by contrast, can be soft on the outside because he is strong on the inside. Through working with his raw edges, confronting his fears, and coming to know himself, he has developed inner potency. This allows him to be gentle and tender with a woman, without feeling emasculated.

Fear of disempowerment by women runs deep in men who, like Samson, have not made friends with the gentler side of their nature. Defining power as conquest, dominance, or an iron will, they fail to recognize their sensitivity as a path that can lead them to their own true nature, where all their inner resources are to be found. Instead, they imagine they are losing strength when they feel open or tender. Feeling threatened by their own sensitivity, they have a hard time opening their hearts to women.

Such narrow, rigid notions of power are less common in cultures where men grow up respecting the earth and are taught to value both sides of their nature. Many Tibetan or Native American leaders, such as the Dalai Lama or Black Elk, embody an integrated strength that is extraordinarily gentle at the same time. This balanced sense of power was also appreciated more fully in the age of chivalry. The first and foremost knight that Merlin installs at King Arthur's Round Table is King Pellinore, because, in Howard Pyle's narrative, "he is both exceedingly gentle of demeanor . . . and at the same time terribly strong and skillful."

Anger and Potency

Another way in which a man may fail to generate real potency is by never developing a healthy relationship with the energy of anger. With thousands of years of hunting and fighting in their background, men are naturally more aggressive than women. Aggression is part of their yang nature. If a man suppresses or rejects this aggressive energy, he becomes what Robert Bly calls a "soft male," lacking in direction and confidence. On the other hand, if he identifies with his anger, mindlessly venting it on others, he remains a peevish little boy or becomes dangerous. A man cannot be truly powerful in his relations with women until he can relate to this yang forcefulness in a conscious, mindful way.

Men often feel guilty about their anger, especially in relation to women. This is understandable, for it is a difficult energy to harness or channel constructively. Also, most of us have not had older male mentors to teach us how to handle our anger skillfully. So after witnessing countless examples of crude male aggression in the media and in the world around us, we come to believe that this energy is intrinsically violent and harmful. Then when we are angry with someone we love, we feel badly about ourselves. Consequently, we squelch the anger, until it finally explodes one day when we can keep it down no longer.

Finding the deeper strength contained in our aggressive energy requires inner attention, inquiry, and perseverance. First we need to remember the truth of coemergence: that all of our feelings and emotions contain a certain intelligence, which we lose sight of when we become swept up in their drama. Understanding this helps us turn and face our anger, as a sign that something is calling for attention. We need to be willing to open to the anger and give it space, instead of either opposing it or feeding it with hostile thoughts. This is difficult at first, and takes practice.

Usually when our anger wants to explode, it is because we are engaged in trying to stuff it away. All it really needs is room to be. So we can learn to contain it externally—refraining from dumping it on others—without having to confine it internally—compressing it into a small space inside us. When we can give this fiery energy all the space it needs in the field of awareness, its explosive charge diminishes because it has nothing to oppose. Then it often settles down, becoming a steady, glowing flame that can illuminate and help clarify the situation we are in.

When we open to our anger, we find that it contains much more than mere aggression. Often we discover a genuine "no" that we have been afraid to acknowledge or communicate directly. Recognizing this can be a very positive step, for every genuine no also implies a genuine yes.

Saying no to dishonesty, for instance, implies saying yes to truth. But when we fail to recognize our no, we usually have a hard time declaring our yes as well. We remain mired in a negative identity as complainer, critic, rebel, or tyrant. And this makes our anger more destructive when it does explode.

So if a man finds himself angrily attacking his partner when she behaves a certain way, he might ask himself, "What is the genuine 'no' I am failing to see and communicate here?" It might be, for example, "I don't want you to act like a little girl with me, and I don't want to be your father." Acknowledging this, instead of acting out his aggression, clears the way for him to express his genuine 'yes': "I want to relate to you man-to-woman, in a full-bodied, powerful way."

In opening to our anger, we also find other feelings underneath it—sorrow, fear, or hurt—that are calling for attention and concern. And if we look still further, we often find, hidden deep within our rage, some long-forgotten longing of the soul that we have given up on, because it was consistently frustrated in the past. Freeing up this desire can help us find direction, especially in times when we feel lost.

Gabriel and his wife, Rebecca, had come to me for counseling because their marriage lacked energy and direction. He often acted in passive-aggressive ways—by not carrying through on agreements or by disappearing in the middle of a conflict, instead of saying what he really felt. He recognized this behavior as part of a larger *modus operandi* in which he always tried to please people, smiling solicitously and going out of his way to win their approval, while never feeling deeply connected with anyone.

Once when I asked Gabriel how he felt about this behavior, he said, "I'm exhausted. All my life, I've prostituted myself to get people's love. I'm a prisoner of pleasing, and I want to break out of this. I'm angry about all the time I've wasted 'making nice.'"

I asked him if he was willing to feel his anger directly. He nodded, and started to breathe more deeply. But this was not easy for him. It brought up fear and sadness: "I'm so reasonable. Nothing of who I really am ever comes across. I was the oldest child in the family, and I had to be responsible for all the other kids. My mother always used to tell me, 'Don't be selfish.'" He started to weep. "I remember how she praised me when I helped out around the house, and how that made me feel all warm and wonderful inside. But when I think about that now, I feel resentful."

"What are you most resentful about?"

"That I always had to jump through hoops to get attention, that I never felt loved just for who I was."

Gabriel was beginning to recognize his deep longing—to be seen and valued in his own right. After many years of frustration, this desire had turned into a smoldering resentment underlying all his efforts to please. Although he had begun to touch this anger, he still did not feel it very deeply. To help him with this, I asked: "How does this affect you right now? What is it like to be the good caretaker, the pleaser, the one who always has to do the right thing to get strokes, the one who never gets angry—the *nice boy*!"

These last two words came out like a taunt, partly because I wanted to goad him a bit, and partly because I too was feeling some anger, in resonance with him, about this setup in my own life. This brought his rage to the surface, and I suggested, "Can you let yourself totally feel the energy of this rage? Can you give it all the space it needs, and let yourself open to that energy, *be* that energy?"

Gabriel was quiet for a long while, feeling it inwardly. When I finally asked him what was going on, he said that he felt centered. He had his hand on his belly.

"What is it like to be centered?"

"It's like I have myself at last. I have a sense of who I am. There's a rod inside me that goes right from my belly down into the ground." He paused for a while, apparently savoring the meaning of what he had just expressed. Then he looked at me and said:

"If you want to taunt me about being a nice boy, I know that's *your* stuff. It's not going to make me budge from this spot. Yes, I can be good, I can be kind, but I am other things as well."

"What other things?"

Gabriel now started giving voice to his genuine no, which he had been out of touch with for so long:

"I'm anger. I'm limits. I'm 'That's enough,' and 'I won't kiss up to you, because I have needs too' . . . The words are disappearing now."

"It doesn't have to have words."

"I like that. I usually try so hard to find the right words."

"What's it like to stay with where you are right now?"

"It's quieter now, yet just as strong."

After a while I invited Gabriel to make contact with Rebecca, sitting next to him. As he looked silently into her eyes, a number of different feelings passed across his face. Finally he took a deep breath, reached out for her hand, and said, "This is the closest I've felt to you in a long time."

The quality of his presence had completely changed since the beginning of the session. At first he had been collapsed in on himself; his resentment about having to please had kept his heart closed. But now he was making contact with his wife in a way that was straightforward and irresistible.

In allowing his anger and going all the way into it, Gabriel had begun to recover an inner strength and fire concealed behind his good-boy facade. And he realized that he could actually contact another person from there, rather than from trying to please or win approval. He was finding his genuine yes.

Men and women both need to learn to work more consciously with their anger, always keeping in mind the crucial distinction between feeling it and identifying with it. If we can open to its raw energy, without fixating on hostile thoughts, we discover in it a fiery intensity, a motive power that can help us overcome obstacles, cut through deceit and pretense, and pursue important aims. And when a man unlocks this strength contained in his anger, he can meet a woman's intensity without having to attack or withdraw.

The male impulse to hunt or pursue, to test endurance, and to relish victories has a beauty all its own. In the first half of life this aggressive energy may take crude forms such as garnering sexual conquests. But later in life, when used in the service of truth or awakening, it can become distilled into spiritual potency. Naropa's teacher, a crazy-wisdom yogi named Tilopa, is said to have stormed the palace of the dakinis, who held the ultimate sacred teachings he sought, and would not relent until they had imparted their wisdom to him. He not only wanted to let these women teach him, *he demanded it*. Chögyam Trungpa, a modern descendent of Tilopa's, once described this humorously as "bankrobbing the dakinis." This is an example of positive aggression, used in the service of sacred vision and purpose.

Receptive openness and grounded strength form an important polarity in male development. Taken together, they give us the capacity to face and handle all the different situations that arise in relationships. Accepting and valuing our sensitivity makes us more responsive to our partner, while being on good terms with our fiery energy helps us stand firm and keep our heart open when we feel challenged. As we discover this larger power, born of the union of softness and strength, we will no longer feel threatened by letting down our guard and embracing the feminine as our other half.

DIALOGUE IIA

Men Relating to Women

I.

This dialogue took place after a talk at a men's center where I presented some of the ideas discussed in the previous chapter. (Bold italics represent comments from women in the audience.)

Even in the most tender, sweet, significant moments with women, I find I'm often asked to do something again, to put out, to please, to come up with something for them. When my lover says, "Tell me I'm beautiful," or "Tell me what you feel," part of me wants to go along with that because she needs it, and another part of me says, "Hey, that's not my job. I don't want to have to make her feel good." So what is appropriate action at that point?

What do you think she's asking for?

"Tell me that you love me. Tell me your feelings—in the way I want, the time frame I want, and the tone of voice I want. Also be true to yourself and say it genuinely."

A bit of a double bind? Well, if she puts expectations on you in a demanding way, she is probably trying to use you to fill some hole in herself.

We're all good enough at marketing and sales to demand things in subtle ways.

Are you objecting to a woman asking anything of you? What's the problem for you?

I just don't get it. I don't get the role that I'm supposed to take on as a man, as a lover. Am I her father? Am I her lover? Am I her friend? Where am I?

So you're not sure of where you stand when she wants something from you. When you ask that question—"Where am I?"—how do you feel?

Curious.

Good. That curiosity is the first step on a path where you start to move into unknown territory.

Yes. But I don't think I should be expected to meet all her needs. . . .

I don't think you should either—I'm not suggesting that. But whether or not we satisfy all of a woman's needs, they do bring us to an edge, an unfamiliar place where we don't feel entirely comfortable. Staying present there calls for a certain heroism.

D. H. Lawrence said that modern men would rather stay wrapped up in their cocoons—their comfortable notions of themselves—than take the risk of looking more deeply inward when they feel challenged by a woman. When a woman asks something from us, it often shakes us up and calls on us to find new reserves and resources inside ourselves.

When I'm at work, I don't have any problem doing what people ask of me, but if my woman asks me for something, I often pull back and feel I have to fend her off. So what you're saying is meaningful to me.

It's important not to see this as just your own personal problem. This is also part of our collective karma as men. For thousands of years men have been used to dominating women, telling them what to do. Maybe this programming even goes back to the apes and their domination hierarchies. So when a woman wants something from us, we often feel at a loss. And since women are often more comfortable expressing feelings than men, when they want us to be more emotionally available, we feel out of our league. We need to be kind to ourselves in these situations, and realize that we're not at fault, that what's happening here is also part of a collective male/female issue. That will help us relax and see what the next step is.

What I'm struggling with as a woman is how to express my needs to men. I run the whole gamut from, "Maybe I should be more soft and yielding, and not insist on anything, maybe I am being too confrontive with this poor guy," to "Maybe it's time to split up because I'm beating my head against the wall, we've been in couples therapy six months, and nothing's changing."

What's the resolution for women? I've worked hard at communicating with my partner in a nondemanding way. I try to make "I-statements" instead of focusing on what he's doing wrong, and I try to soften my tone. I think I'm doing everything right. I'm really trying.

I believe you.

Thank you. But I'm beginning to think that maybe I need to leave a relationship sooner when I've tried everything and my needs are still not being met. I hate doing that, I don't want to be alone. But maybe some male egos are not comfortable with my level of energy.

That may be true.

Sometimes the whole thing seems so hopeless.

Yet no matter how bad it seems, if you can open to what you're feeling in the hopelessness—a certain grief, fear, or anger perhaps—that will put you in touch with the real issue for you here. That's the beginning of finding your path—what is right for you in the situation.

Men also need to learn to stay connected with themselves when they hit their wall of hopelessness, when they say to themselves: "I don't know what she wants. I don't know how to give her what she wants. This is all too much for me. I can never give enough. And what I do give is never good enough." When we hit that wall, instead of either trying to please the woman or refusing to give her what she wants, we could feel the raw edge that is being touched inside us. That will help us stay present, which is where we will find the resources we need.

I'd like to hear from you as a woman what is happening for you when you ask things like, "Tell me I'm beautiful, tell me you love me, or tell me how you feel."

What I often find missing in my communication with men is a heartfelt quality, a language of feelings. That is the language I live in. To have a relationship with someone who doesn't speak that tongue, and who doesn't see the value of it, feels like being colorblind, or like seeing a movie without the soundtrack. I'm willing to learn the language of men, but I want a man to be willing to learn my language as well, to be conversant in it, so that our relationship is not just one-dimensional. I need to know that I can invite a man to step into another world and that he would value that.

You say that you're learning the language of men, but I'm curious about what you think the language of men is. For example, there's a real difference in the way that men and women communicate their caring. I often express my caring through actions rather than words. Maybe action is our language. Sometimes it's hard for my partner to appreciate that. For instance, she tends to underdress, and I always carry a jacket for her when we go out, but she usually doesn't appreciate that this is my way of expressing caring. It's not enough. I have to keep telling her, "You're beautiful, I really care for you."

You might try taking that situation as a mirror: If your woman is always wanting to know if you love her, maybe this also reflects something going on inside you. Is it possible that your feminine side is also needing more attention, more cherishing, more recognition from you?

On the inner level, if men don't value their yin nature—the tender, sweet, delicate part of themselves— this makes it hard for them to cherish a woman. Maybe it's appropriate sometimes for a man to praise and adore the lovely qualities of a woman. Maybe when she asks for that, it's not just an ego trip on her part. Maybe it's fitting for the yang in a man to radiate appreciation and for the yin in a woman to receive that, just as it may be fitting for the yin in a woman to admire and respect a man's yang strength. Maybe this is part of the *lila*—the sacred play—between men and women. Maybe a man can only learn from a woman, and receive the teachings she has to offer, when he honors her like this.

Yet when a woman asks for this, a man will feel disempowered if he sees himself as a child whose mother is nagging him to be thoughtful and considerate. If we can pay attention to what is happening inside us at these moments, instead of just projecting and reacting, then we can speak our truth, instead of feeling resentful or compromised. For example, we might tell our partner, "Here's what's true for me: When you ask me to tell you I love you, I hear that as a demand. Maybe that's not how you mean it, but that's how I take it. And then I wind up feeling trapped and claustrophobic. I want you to know I love you, but I need to let you know that in a way that feels spontaneous and authentic."

But what if a woman wants me to be in my heart, and I just don't feel that way? Maybe she made me feel bad yesterday and I don't want to tell her I love her today. If I say that to her, she's not going to understand me any more than I can understand her need for me to be in my heart.

What's she not going to understand?

You're saying that when she wants something, I need to get down, speak from my insides, and respond to her in an honest way. But that's not always going to be what she wants to hear.

Possibly, but how can you be so sure?

I've been married twice.

Why would she not want to hear what's true for you?

How do I know? Ask the women.

No, you've been married twice—tell me.

Because the woman is asking for something that I am not good at communicating.

I understand what you're saying. But it also sounds like you're hardening your position and making a solid identity out of it. Maybe you're reacting out of a belief that you are deficient in this area—and that keeps you from being willing to explore new territory.

If you have a hard time expressing feelings, you could at least start by acknowledging that, instead of making a woman wrong for what she wants. If you can be honest about your struggle, she will often respond and love you for that, even if you are not giving her what she initially asked for. At least some real meeting is taking place—and that is what she wants, ultimately. A woman wants to feel a man's energy in contact with hers.

A woman wants to know that we can be present—*as ourselves,* and *with her.* Her way of saying that might be, "Tell me more about your feelings." But what she's really asking is, "Are you here?" If we can say, "Yes, I'm here," the rest will probably work itself out.

Often when a woman expresses some desire or frustration, a man's initial response is to think, "Oh, my God, how can I make her feel better? How can I fix this for her?" But when we try to fix what is happening, we move into the busy, controlling part of our mind and leave our heart behind, which only makes things worse.

Some men who have had bad experiences opening themselves to women have concluded, "Women *say* they want you to show them your feelings, but when you do, then they don't respect you." That can happen sometimes, especially if the woman feels threatened by the man's feelings. But I have not found this to be generally true, either personally or in working with couples. When it does happen, it's often because a man has become totally *identified* with his feelings, or overwhelmed by them, instead of simply acknowledging them. Though he's expressing his feelings, he's lost his ground and is not really present in himself. And *being present*—rather than *being emotional*—is what allows real intimacy to happen.

I'd suggest that you try sharing your truth with your partner, instead of reacting so defensively. Then you might discover that *that* is what she really wants to hear.

But it seems like she can never get enough of it.

That's right! That's right, nobody can get enough of it—real connection, based on being genuine and truthful.

It's just that we go at it in different ways.

That's right. So what's the problem?

Women know what they feel. And they have no trouble talking personally with each other, even if they're complete strangers. Men don't do that. Maybe we're starting to, but we don't allow ourselves to do that.

Right! That's the whole point: *We don't allow ourselves to do it.* If we don't know what we feel, it's often because we don't let ourselves listen to the pulse of life flowing deep within us. Can you imagine a world where most men cherished and tuned into their inner life? Can you imagine how that would change everything?

When we open to our inner reality, we discover a deep wellspring inside us. A man who is cut off from his inner feminine is dry. That's why men often have a hard time talking to each other—we're so dry inside. When we open to the inner feminine, there's a warmth, and moistening, and fullness that wells up, like an oasis in a desert.

When our yang strength works in partnership with that delicacy and tenderness, we develop a much deeper power than the dry, brittle hardness of men who are cut off from their inner life. This is the inner marriage and communion that our world so desperately needs.

II.

This dialogue took place at the end of a five-day couples workshop. The men and women had just finished talking among themselves separately, before coming back together again. The men sat on one side of the room facing the women on the other side. Like two halves of a Greek chorus, members of each group began expressing their feelings, desires, and concerns to the other, back and forth.

F: *I'm afraid that if I'm completely who I am, I'll overwhelm you, like a steamroller, and you will run away. So I often give up my power when I'm around you.*

M: *What am I supposed to do about that?*

F: *Nothing. Nothing.*

M: *Then go the next step with me. Having said that, what do you expect to happen?*

F: *Nothing. I just want you to listen to me.*

M: *And just do nothing?*

F: *Just hear it.*

M: *But if you're giving up your power because of me, I imagine it's going to come back at me somehow. That's anxiety-provoking, so I feel like I should do something about it.*

F: *Often when I don't claim my power, I project on men that they're taking it away from me. But I want to acknowledge here that men don't get in the way of my power. It's my belief in my limitations that takes away my power. There's a lot of confusion about what female power is. So if you men are afraid of losing your power, it's true over here, too. It's true all over. It's part of being human.*

M: *It has been powerful for me to realize that my deepest fear is that I will be inadequate. I don't think I am inadequate, but I often fear that I am. And when I feel pressure from my partner to do something like reveal my feelings, it stirs up this fear that I'm not going to be able to do it. I don't want her to think that I am inadequate.*

F: *I feel frustrated when confronted with your fear of inadequacy. That's not how I see things. I only ask you to be with me, to share the journey. I don't expect perfection. Just be present with me. Maybe that sounds like a demand, but I don't want you to hear my invitation to join me in life as a demand that's going to trigger a feeling of inadequacy. I don't like feeling inadequate myself—I know how that feels. I want you to know that I can live with your weaknesses as well as my own.*

M: *Deep inside me, I'm not sure I believe that you can live with my weaknesses. I'm afraid that if you see my weak points, you will turn away in disgust.*

F: *I feel very touched when you're willing to show me your weak points. I am overjoyed that you would reveal yourself like that. It makes me feel closer to you and more in love with you.*

M: *I don't want to be loved for my weaknesses, really. Am I only worth something when I show my feelings and emotions? If I am not recognized for my power and my adequacies and for the things I feel good about, then I'm lost. And I don't know what I have to offer you.*

F: *You're most genuine to me, though, when you get in touch with the raw place in you where you're not sure, where you're not trying to maintain an image of what you think you should be. Then I feel like I can connect with you. I can't connect to the part of you that has to be knowledgeable and competent all the time. I connect more with the part of you that's just beginning to find its way and doesn't quite have it all together yet.*

M: *But can you hear what I am saying about this? Maybe what you're saying seems true to you—that you can connect with us most when we're feeling raw. But it's painful that what I'm proudest of, you often can't connect with and even despise. It sounds like you're saying, "We love you when you're weak and vulnerable. We don't love you when you're fully yourself and in your power."*

M: *It seems ironic that you say you can love your partner most when he expresses his inadequacy. What he as a man loves most about himself is his competence.*

F: *We didn't say that. We never said that.*

M: *But I often hear it that way. I understand what you're saying about being raw, but the other side is that when I'm feeling best about myself, I often get the message, "You're being a little too rough or too full of yourself," rather than, "Look at that energy, isn't it beautiful." It often seems that I'm loved more for revealing weakness—though on another level I know it's not really weakness—than for being strong. That feels unbalanced to me.*

F: *I feel strong right now and really excited. Because you're saying these things to us, all of you, in a really direct and honest way. That feels exciting.*

F: *The words* weakness *and* strength *aren't really what it's about for me. I'm not looking for someone who's either strong or weak. I'm looking for someone who's honest and whose integrity I can respect. I want to be with someone whose strength is his integrity and his ability to be forthright—honest when he feels strong and honest when he feels weak. That's strength.*

F: *Honesty is the strength. Truth—that's the strength.*

M: *My problem is that I'm not even sure what genuine strength looks like. Out of all of the men here, only two felt they had good* relationships with their fathers. The rest of us didn't have a role model of what real power looks like. We're trying to learn, but we're stuck with the John Wayne stereotype. So whatever we do, we're reaching, and learning, and yearning for ourselves.

F: *I want to be able to love you even if you can't always be honest. But sometimes I have no patience because I'm so needy myself.*

M: *I have a lot of pain about a lost boyhood, a boyhood that never happened, and a lot of pain about a father who never provided a real model of how to be a man. I feel a hole inside me because of that. In talking together as men, we never once mentioned our mothers—our sense of loss around our fathers was that powerful.*

F: *It helps me to hear that. It's good to know that it's not just your connection with your mothers that is so distorted.*

And I understand that you don't want to become feminized. I respect that a lot. I want to know you as you, the maleness of you. I hear that you're not sure of what that might be, that you don't have good role models. But as I sit here and I feel you, I know you're very different from me. I want to know more about what that difference is. I don't want you to become just like me.

I'm aware that it's tempting to ask all of you to join me in a language that I'm comfortable with. I really need to learn how to speak your language too—whether that means joining you in projects or doing the things you do so well. I don't believe that women are the experts at relationship.

I feel good around you when I know that you're proud of yourself. I hear that you also want to feel that as men, but you're not quite sure how to get in touch with it. I'd like to hear more about what you're proud of in being men.

M: *The main thing we want to offer—though we are not too sure of being able to do it, and it's something we are working on as part of our path—is a vision of what's possible . . . providing leadership, focus, patience, perseverance, stability . . . and taking risks.*

M: *Since I grew up with an absent father, one thing I feel good about is making physical contact with my children, especially my boys. I like to hug them, tussle with them. For me that's a way of being close with my boys. But sometimes when we horse around in the kitchen, it seems to frighten my wife or push her buttons. I'm going to do that whether she likes it or not, but it makes me wonder why women have a hard time with that male boisterousness.*

F: *I like watching men play. Recently I had the honor of presenting a program to Rotary Club members, all men. I don't know if I'd ever been with a hundred men in a room before. I felt high. There was a lot of energy, a lot of power, and a lot of fun happening there. It was great.*

M: *The whole conversation so far has been about what it is to be a man. All we seem to have on this end are questions like, "What are we?" That's because we're not sure what the hell we are. I feel like we're a gender in process. We've been so busy for so many years reacting to your revolution, and trying to relate to how you're changing, and trying to see if we can be in sync with what you want us to be, that we've lost sight of what it is we are.*

And now we don't know whether the way we were was any good, or whether what we're becoming is better, or what the hell we are. We don't know where we're going or how to get there. We need our direction to come from ourselves. We don't want to define ourselves in reaction to you. But you're so present that it's hard not to.

F: *I can understand what you're saying because we are changing too. I sometimes fear that if I really go into my power, I'll lose my femininity. This has nothing to do with my husband not wanting me to take my power, because when I am in my power, he loves it, he really enjoys it. But there's still a part of me that's frightened to move into this new way of being. It's scary for me.*

M: *Though we're not really sure how to be men sometimes, and what that means, what we're sure of is that we don't want to be women.*

F: *We don't always know what it is to be women, either. We do know that we don't want to be men.*

M: *I feel a lot of trust in this process we're going through right now. It's like we're all saying, "Well, we don't know." Great—we don't know. That gives us room to experiment, to share and connect with each other in that uncertainty, and see what it is that wants to come forth. One thing's certain, though—we can't go back. I can't go back and get something from my father that he never gave me. I have to find that here and now. We're holding a powerful energy in doing this.*

So there are two possibilities. On the one hand we could say, "I don't know what it is to be a man, so there must be something wrong with me. I must be inadequate if I don't know what I'm supposed to be." Or we could say, "I don't know what it is to be a man because I'm in process." *That's* an important part of being a man—being willing to explore new possibilities, playing the edge, continually rediscovering what it is to be a man. Since life is always evolving, why shouldn't our gender be in process, evolving as well?

F: *What John just said makes me realize that women are in process too. The women's movement has given me great strength as an individual but it hasn't taught me how to be in a relationship with a man. In fact, it's made that really difficult. Sometimes I wish I were in my mother's generation because those are the skills I learned about how to be in a relationship. My fears about relationship tell me that I'm still in process too.*

M: *When we grew up as boys and as young men we didn't talk to each other about our feelings. We talked about who won the ball game, or what girl we were going out with, or what was going on with the car. But we didn't say what it was like to be going through adolescence, or how it felt to not fit in with the other guys, or to be punished by our dad for something we didn't do. We usually didn't talk like that. So when you ask us how we feel about something, there's not much to draw on. Because we never expressed our feelings while we were growing up.*

F: *What did you do with the feelings, then?*

M: *We swallowed them.*

M: *This is a very important thing we're discussing. We really need for you to hear this. That's why we think of talking about feelings as a female kind of thing. We have the feelings, but we don't know how to put them into words. I have had very strong feelings during the last three days. I've had hair sticking up on my arm and have been really emotional. But I can't tell you what those feelings were. I know I've been on the edge. But I can't describe it with words. When I'm expected to express it in words and can't, then I have that personal fear of inadequacy.*

F: *Well, maybe my mother was right many years ago when she said that the woman's role is to protect the male ego. . . .*

M: *I'm sorry, I don't want my ego protected.*

F: *I want to say something to men about this. I really see and honor your kind of power and the gifts you have to offer me. And I want you to be able to recognize and honor the gifts that we can offer you, and the places where we may be ahead of you in our development. I want you to be able to see and honor that in us without referring it back to questions of your adequacy——whether it emasculates you or not. Our distortion is that sometimes we're demanding about how we want you to grow, sometimes our ego takes over when we do that. And yet there's a genuine truth here too——there are areas where we have special gifts and we're your teachers. And I want you to be able to honor that in us.*

M: *What are the strengths you honor in us?*

F: *I love your male vision. I love your male power. I love your aggressive animal sexuality. I love your capacity to bring through a larger impersonal wisdom. That totally turns me on. I have no problem in giving that my reverence.*

And I need you to be able to give me your reverence for my particular powers, without feeling like that emasculates you.

M: *Could you explain what you meant by being developmentally ahead of us? That brought up a feeing of inadequacy.*

F: *I acknowledge the ways that you as men are developed in ways I'm not. And I acknowledge you as my teachers in those areas. But I also want you to be able to see how I may be developed in ways that you aren't. I want you to be willing to acknowledge where I might be your teacher, without immediately becoming competitive about it, or worrying about how that makes you inadequate, or feeling that I'm trying to emasculate you.*

M: *I want to acknowledge that I hear what you're saying, and that I'm grateful for it. I want to be open, and learn what women have to teach.*

Yet at the same time it does bring up some fear, right? For a man in our culture, learning from a woman often feels threatening.

F: *I'm a little concerned about the idea of "developmentally more advanced." I want to be careful not to say that one gender or the other is superior. You have your gifts, and we have our gifts. That doesn't mean that one strength is better than the other. It simply means that we can appreciate the strength in the other sex that we've never developed in ourselves.*

M: *Okay, I'll use the dirty words: My partner is "developmentally more advanced" than I am in the area of intimacy and communicating about it, talking about feelings, and helping me explore inner realms where I have never gone before. That doesn't feel like a threat or an indictment. I'm grateful for that. I'm glad she complements me that way.*

M: *I have a deep-seated fear that you will grow tired of being my teacher, that you will become impatient and go elsewhere because you think I'll never learn. I want to let you know that I'm still strug-*

gling to learn more about what you bring into my life. I don't know how to express this to you, but I am working on it. And I ask you to be patient.

M: *I'm terribly afraid of hurting you. I feel incapable of not doing that, and I feel frustrated about it. My great fear is that I am leading you to some emotional catastrophe.*

F: *I don't want you trying to make everything okay for me. I just want you to look at yourself and work with yourself. And that's what I want to do too. What I often hear is, "No matter what I do, you're not happy." I don't want you to try to second-guess my happiness. Just find your own happiness. Be yourself, and allow me to do the same.*

M: *I have a hard time staying in touch with my own vision. When I get all caught up in what a woman wants, and seeing how I'm not filling her needs, that tells me I've lost my own sense of vision.*

M: *One area where you as women seem more advanced is in your ability to touch your pain, and to hang out with not having to do something about it. We are just coming to the point where we can acknowledge our pain and suffering.*

F: *Maybe that's one way we can be your teacher.*

M: *If you can teach from the heart, maybe we can learn from that. But if you try to get us to be like you, that's not what we're looking for.*

We often feel that we learn to become men by becoming involved with women. But that's not the answer either. You can teach us a lot, but you can't teach us how to be men. Teach us by being who you are, not by telling us what to do.

F: *Exactly.*

M: *I often end up feeling that women make a value judgment that the feminine track—the areas where women are more developed—is a better track, a higher track, a more worthwhile track than the areas where I feel more skilled and more advanced.*

Instead of focusing on the other gender at this point, maybe we could bring in more fourfold truth here—not just voicing concerns, but also acknowledging the distortions that block real communication.

F: *One distortion of ours is not always knowing how to be teachers from our being and our heart without getting it mixed up in our ego and our own agenda. That's where we are as human beings. And so we're learning. We have to grow into that.*

F: *In my heart, it pains me to acknowledge that. In my heart, that's painful.*

One of our distortions is in thinking there's something wrong with us when we feel pain. So we cover it up and pretend that everything's okay. "How are you feeling?" "Hey, I'm really cool. I'm fine." And that makes it hard for us to stay open to you or learn from you.

M: *As guys growing up we always played games that had rules. But in relationships with women, we don't know what the rules are— they keep on changing. So we don't know how to play. If we knew there was Rule Number One, Two, Three, then we could play better.*

But having a rule is a good way to avoid being on an edge. That's part of our cop-out—trying to find some rule for how we should be. "If we just figure out the rules, then we'll be okay, we'll be able to master the situation." That's another distortion.

M: *John, maybe some of us need the safety of that in order to be able to experiment. I feel like you're setting up a rule by saying there can't be any rules.*

I'm not saying there can't be any rules. Couples need ground rules sometimes. I'm saying that one of my distortions is to look for some external standard to measure up to, in order to make myself feel safe, to convince myself that I know what I'm doing. It's a cop-out when I do that.

M: *Yes. Where's the rawness of the heart?*

F: *Right. Part of my distortion is expecting men to tell me the rules. My father always laid down the rules. And it seems like men have drafted most of the rules that govern our world. So I imagine that men are supposed to know. That belief is still in me, and it's painful to admit.*

F: *What I want from my relationships is genuineness. All human beings have feelings, whether they're men or women. But when your feelings don't come through, I begin to lose trust in you. I begin to feel you aren't genuine. And then I begin doubting myself as well. It's scary for me when there's pretense. I need to know that you see the value in intimate relationship, and that you're willing to learn more about how to be genuine in your relations with us.*

M: *We give you pretense because we're scared to death of our feelings. We are struggling with how to be authentic as men.*

F: *We hear that.*

M: *We keep up facades not just with you, but with each other as men as well. Women love men and men love women, but I wish that men loved men more than they do. We have a lot of fear of each other as men. We've got to go beyond that by being stronger, which means really caring about one another and revealing our vulnerability at the same time. Men have to learn how to love men if we are to love ourselves as individuals. Then we can love women in a much wholer way.*

M: *It's much easier to open up with a woman who encourages us to be tender than it is with another man who might not respect that tender place in us.*

F: *Is that the feeling that you had with your fathers—that they cut you off when you were feeling vulnerable?*

Our fathers generally didn't allow themselves to feel their own pain. Their lack of connection with their own feeling-life made it hard for us to connect with them, and therefore with ourselves.

F: *You know, I haven't heard what anyone has said for the last few minutes because I've been feeling so full inside.*

When I was young I grew up believing that men were more knowledgeable and better at most things than women. Then as I grew older, I spent many years discounting men. I would walk into a room and find most of the women there interesting, while most of the men didn't appeal to me at all.

What I became aware of here just now was that regardless of what you men were saying, I could look across at all of you and feel that there was not one of you I didn't find interesting, not one I would not enjoy spending some time with. I could feel your struggle and your honesty, and that opened something up in me.

It feels delightful to discover that I could begin to open again to a whole class of people that I had discounted! I really value and appreciate you for this, and myself for letting this happen. That feels really good to me.

Let us end at this point with each side making a bow to the other.

Chapter Twelve

SUCHNESS AND MAGIC

*Always search for your innermost
nature in those you are with.*

RUMI

As lovers join their lives together, they inevitably start falling into routines. They develop roles, predictable ways of reacting to each other, familiar nuances and insinuations, all based on the assumption, "I know who you are." Although it feels comforting to know and be known, this familiarity can also start to drain the juice out of the relationship. After a while, one or both partners start dreaming of other lovers—people they *don't* already know, and who don't already know them. They want their freedom back—their freedom from the known, their beginner's mind.

What Do We Really Love in Another?

When my relationship starts to feel too familiar, it is helpful to reconsider what it is I really love about my partner. Is it her body? Yes, her body pleases me, and I am drawn to the ways it moves, feels, smells, and tastes. Yet if her body were suddenly to fall ill or start to fail, I might not find it as pleasing, but I would still love her nonetheless. So if it's not her body I love, perhaps it's the way she is in her body. But who is the "she" that inhabits this body?

Is it her personality? Her personality is what I know. It pleases me in some ways, aggravates me in other ways. Our two personalities do a dance with each other, which is sometimes enjoyable, sometimes painful. I have become attached to her personality in certain ways, as I have to her body. Yet if our interaction is confined to this level, it eventually grows tiresome; it does not lead to greater expansiveness or depth. No, the one I most love is not a personality.

What I love in her speaks and moves in silence. It is something that lives behind the facades of body and personality. Or is it rather something that lives *in* her body and personality? Contemplating this draws me into the mystery of being.

Of course, I could cut this inquiry short with a ready answer: Her soul, that's what I love about her! But *soul* at this point is only a word, a concept, an explanation—it doesn't really tell me anything. Can we really say what soul *is*, after all? It's a word we use to name the unnameable.

The term *soul* is useful because it belongs to common parlance and has many rich overtones and associations. But that is also the problem with it. I can say, "I love her soul," and assume that I know what I am talking about. But in truth, I have no idea what this so-called soul that I love really is. Looking into her eyes, I cannot help but wonder, "What is this you-ness that makes you *you*?" This "you" that I love is much deeper and vaster than your conditioned personality, yet also more singular and distinctive than you-as-pure-being. Here is where, if we have to use a word at all for the mystery of embodied being, I prefer one that preserves this mystery—*suchness*. Suchness means *just so*.

Just So

What I love about my beloved is that she is *just so*. Her particular quality of *just so* is not something that can be pinned down. At each moment she is just so in a slightly different way. Her way of being herself, just so, is forever changing, and finding new expression. It unfolds like a dance, sometimes hot, sometimes sweet.

Sometimes I study her when she is not looking to see if I can detect who she *really* is. Yet this only deepens my state of unknowing. When I try to grasp her suchness, it slips through my fingers like water. To appreciate who she really is, in herself, I must approach her with the utmost delicacy, as D. H. Lawrence suggests:

Whoever wants life must go softly towards life, softly as one would go towards a deer and a fawn that was nestling under a tree. One gesture of violence, one violent assertion of self-will and life is gone.... But with quietness, with an abandon of self-assertion and a fullness of the deep, true self one can approach another human being, and know the delicate best of life, the touch.

The Japanese poet Basho also describes how we need to approach the mystery of suchness when he writes:

> *From the pine tree*
> *learn of the pine tree*
> *And from the bamboo*
> *of the bamboo.*

Commenting on these verses, the Japanese philosopher Nishitani explains that Basho does not mean

> that we should "observe the pine tree carefully." Still less does he mean for us to "study the pine tree scientifically." He means for us to enter the mode of being where the pine tree is the pine tree itself, and the bamboo is the bamboo itself, and from there to look at the pine tree and the bamboo. He calls on us to betake ourselves to the dimension where things become manifest in their suchness.

This is the realm where, as Martin Buber writes, "The tree is no longer an *It*," an object of my thought or observation. To learn of the pine tree from the pine tree is to enter into its presence, its way of being, and to be fully present there myself.

And so we could say, following Lawrence and Basho, "From your beloved, learn of the beloved. Enter into her presence. Giving up your attempts to know her, meet her with your own presence. Then you may catch a glimpse of who she really is."

To meet my beloved in her suchness is to experience her as pure Thou, as *sacred Other*. In such moments when I tell her, "I love you," I am saying, "My whole being responds to you in this place where you are wholly you. I enter into the sacred space where you are just so and none other. I am a guest here in your home-ground."

At the absolute level—of pure being, pure spirit—my beloved and I are one. Yet at the relative level—of embodied being—we are forever distinctly two. And in many ways our twoness is an even greater mystery than our oneness. How can I possibly understand that the divine principle at work in the universe has taken just this form, that it embodies itself as *her*, so different from me?

This is where the death of a loved one causes the deepest grief. Though if she died I might be able to love again, no one else could ever touch and stir me in the way that she does. Her nature opens for me a unique window, and unveils a particular view, which no one else could ever reveal in the same way. Despite all the spiritual teachings about nonattachment, the truth is that our souls are linked.

Reentering the Sacred Ground

At times, however, my partner and I stray from this deeper kind of connecting, as our old, familiar personality patterns take over. Then I react once again to her surfaces—seeing her as an object *to have* or *to do* something with. "This is the exalted melancholy of our fate," writes Buber, "that every Thou in our world must become an It." We cannot avoid this fate, this fall into separateness, where we make ourselves and everything we most love into an object of our thought, our scrutiny, our designs. An ongoing relationship continually tends to stray from the sacred play of I/Thou into the conventional drama of self/Other."

Of course, as soon as I treat my partner as a collection of known habits and characteristics, this immediately imprisons me in my own personality as well. Rumi warns of this, speaking from the beloved's perspective: "If you try to define and narrow me, you will only starve yourself of yourself." Yet if I can recognize and feel this starvation as it comes upon me, it also brings back my holy hunger—to dwell in the sacred ground once more, where she and I are fully alive with each other, in our sacred oneness and our sacred otherness.

What I love in my partner, then, is nothing I can ever grasp or hold on to. I can only glimpse her suchness in fleeting moments, and continually rediscover it anew. I come to know her as she is only when I give up thinking that I know her.

Recognizing the unfathomable nature of what I love keeps bringing me back to the mystery of being. When I meet my partner in her home-ground, I return home at the same time. I am myself again, the real I, which overflows the boundaries of name and form. This is love's magic.

Chapter Thirteen

DISAPPOINTMENT, DEVOTION, AND GROWING UP

Expectations are never fulfilled. If you expect, then you are in bondage. Not having expectations is your true nature.

H. L. POONJA

Loving someone passionately stirs up deep longings for fulfillment, but if we expect a relationship to provide satisfaction that we cannot otherwise find within us, we set ourselves up for disappointment. Disillusion sets in when we realize that our partner is an imperfect, struggling mortal like ourselves; when we find that loving and passionate feelings do not remain constant; or when the relationship never quite manages to yield the ultimate happiness we had hoped for. Even if our partner is everything we could ever want, and our connection a real treasure, this can never in itself provide complete fulfillment.

The Gates of Hell

As lovers grow closer, they often fall into an unconscious collusion: "I'll fill up your holes and compensate you for the ways you're incomplete, and you do the same for me." In this way, they create a codependent state where each of them feels both taken care of and needed. Yet in looking to another person to fill our holes, we create a parent/child setup. We see ourselves as an undeveloped or wounded child, and our partner as the good parent who should give us what we never received when we were young: perfect love, validation, mirroring, or support.

Whenever we expect another person to make us whole, we set ourselves in opposition to reality. Then when our partner inevitably fails to live up to this expectation, we start to plunge into hell, because we have lost our own ground. Buddhist psychology describes hell as a state of mind ruled by hatred and rejection of things as they are. Struggling to get out of hell only makes it worse, for this is just another way of rejecting where we are. The only way out of hell is through opening and listening to our disappointment.

Disappointment always contains a powerful and accurate message that can be trusted: We have placed our longing where it doesn't really belong. If we can hear what our disillusionment is trying to tell us, it brings us down to earth and helps us recognize *the truth of what is*. Such moments of recognition provide major opportunities for growing up, for moving forward in our development. Seen in this light, disappointment is an important stepping-stone on the path of conscious relationship.

Opportunities for Growing Up

Here is where disappointment can become an ally: It wakes us from our trance, where we are locked in the mindset of a needy child seeking love outside to provide the fulfillment we lack inside. At first it seems painful to acknowledge our disillusionment, for it brings up deep feelings of loss, hunger, or grief. The emptiness we encounter here is an old, familiar feeling: It is the abyss we have been trying to fill with relationships all our life.

This feeling of emptiness is especially painful when we imagine it means that love and fulfillment do not belong to us, and that we need to get them from someone else, who is currently failing to provide them. As children we really did need others' love in order to develop confidence in our basic goodness. And while we may still need acknowledgment and caring, if we always expect *others* to provide these, instead of finding them within ourselves, we remain as a child in our relationships.

To remain as a child means seeing Other—our lover, the world, money, position, success—as the provider of nourishment which self must acquire in order to survive. To grow up means making a crucial transition—from a life focused on extracting as much as we can from Other, to a life of creativity and love, which flow naturally from our essential being. This requires a shift in our sense of who we are—*from the false self, whose identity is based on old setups from the past, to the true self, whose nature is an ongoing openness to what is.*

Ego—the known, familiar image of "me," the self-concept that tells me who I am—is what the child-mind fabricated to provide orientation and security in an uncertain world. If we continue to buy this view of ourselves, we pay the price of imprisonment in the past, for the known "me" is always constructed out of old self/Other setups.

Instead, we need to find and manifest our *true* individuality—the living I, which is not a known concept, but a creative presence forever unfolding in new and unforeseen ways. This is the real growing up that needs to happen.

Since opening to our disappointment or emptiness does not feed the ego, it provides a step toward growing up. Yet as we turn toward these feelings, we may encounter a host of demons—primitive fears and stories from the past—that stand in the way. At this point it is important to realize that these fears belong to the child: "Yes, it is the child in me who is starving for recognition ... who wants others to always be there when he needs them ... who sees love as something *out there* ... who imagines that his pain is bigger than he is, and that it will destroy him if he opens to it ... " Naming the child-identity and its beliefs in this way calls forth our larger, reflective awareness. And this allows us to make room for the hunger, panic, or despair we could never let ourselves feel as a child—without becoming overwhelmed by them. In this way, we start to loosen our old identification with the child.

As we move through the whirlwind of primitive fears and beliefs surrounding our disappointment and emptiness, it is like entering the eye of a hurricane. Here at the center of the storm, we are no longer swirling around in confusion, trying to escape from ourselves. As we relate more directly to our experience, our sadness seems more like tenderness, while our emptiness feels like expansive, open space.

Returning to Source

This larger openness, which feels like vast space, is understood in many spiritual traditions as the very core of consciousness, the pure source from which all positive human qualities arise. When we don't resist it, we find nothing here to fear. Instead, we discover what we have been looking for all along—a sense of fullness and depth where we naturally feel good, and at peace with ourselves. This is the wish-fulfilling gem from which all blessings flow. Once my wife, Jennifer, in such a moment of self-remembering, found this poem arising in her:

> *The jewel inside has grown dusty.*
> *What out there could have captured you so*
> *That you forgot all about this one?*
> *Feel the tragedy of that error.*
> *And see: Even now, the tears of your grief*
> *Are washing the dust away.*

This jewel of open presence is what we lost as children, out of fear, not recognizing it as the source of love and awakening. And we continue to feel the consequences of this loss—as the anxious sense of lack we carry inside us, the dead spot, the hole, the abyss we try to fill with relationships, money, or worldly success. Until we are willing to face and enter this abyss, we will never discover that *here* is where we will find the treasure we lost long ago.

And so, when we can finally remain present in the middle of that seeming desert where we feel empty and unfulfilled, the water of new life unexpectedly springs forth. Antonio Machado describes this in one of his poems as a "spring breaking out inside my heart":

> *Along what secret aqueduct,*
> *Oh water, are you coming to me now,*
> *Water of a new life*
> *that I have never drunk before?*

This water of new life—which tastes pure and fresh because it flows from the "secret aqueduct," the underground springs, the unconditioned source—is what we have been thirsting for all these years.

When we arrive at this deep source underneath our disappointment, things no longer seem so bad after all. We are no longer in hell. We have been thoroughly tenderized by the failure of our attempts to control reality. And this allows us simply to appreciate what *is* here—just being, feeling present and open, while also letting our partner just be, without expectations.

In such moments, when we let go of trying to grasp fulfillment *out there*, we experience something that all the sacred traditions regard as an essential step on the path of awakening—renunciation. According to Chögyam Trungpa, renunciation means letting down the barrier between self and Other,

> making yourself more available, more gentle and open to others. The warrior who has accomplished true renunciation is completely naked and raw. He has no desire to manipulate situations. He is able to be, quite fearlessly, what he is. The result of [this] letting go is that [he] discover[s] a bank of self-existing energy that is always available. It is the energy of basic goodness.

Devotion for the Beloved

This kind of letting go usually happens only after a long, futile struggle to bend reality to our will. When our attempts to extract fulfillment from our partner lie shattered, broken open on the hard rocky ground of disappointment, the deeper object of our longing—which is *no* object, nothing Other at all—can make itself known. The Beloved we most long to join with is the mysterious power and wisdom of the universe flowing through us, animating and illuminating our soul.

Feeling devotion toward *this* Beloved is what draws it

closer to us. Only when we are devoted to realizing our own true nature, with the intensity and passion we usually reserve for romantic pursuits, will we find the ultimate fulfillment we seek. Only when we are at-one with ourself will our life be full, rich, and deep. "To find the Beloved," as Rumi points out, "you must *become* the Beloved."

In the first half of life we tend to seek outside ourselves for the source of love and fulfillment. This is what draws us to a lover or a spiritual teacher. He or she seems to radiate something precious and marvelous, a depth and richness we have rarely glimpsed before. But if we become too dazzled by a spiritual master, we miss the true meaning of the work—which is to discover who we really are. And if we look to a lover for fulfillment, the jewel inside only grows more dusty, leaving us feeling all the more dissatisfied.

It is only when we become disenchanted with this project—of projecting our own greatness out there—that we awaken to the deeper meaning of love—as an encounter with the sacred presence that lies at the heart of our being and at the heart of the world. Intimate relationship is the outer reflection of this secret love affair.

An Alliance of Warriors

When I no longer put what is essentially a spiritual longing on my partner, this frees her of a great burden—to make my life work, to fill up my abyss, to be the instrument of my salvation. It also frees me to see and love her as a real person, and to appreciate the real gifts she brings into my life. So as my devotional energy moves freely toward its deepest aim, it naturally infuses our relationship as well. I feel more devoted to my partner's well-being and *her* deepest unfolding; I want her inner jewel to sparkle too.

When two partners move in this direction, they leave behind the old parent/child dynamic—"I'll take care of you, and you take care of me." And they forge a much deeper bond, based on encouraging each other to honor the sacred presence and basic goodness within them. This is a relationship between true adults, one that can allow for old feelings from childhood, without being driven by them. Then two lovers can appreciate their connection for what it is—not as heaven or hell on earth, but as an alliance of warriors, a loving communion of two fellow travelers on the path.

Chapter Fourteen

THE BROKEN-HEARTED
WARRIOR AND THE
RENEWAL OF THE WORLD

Why, then, have to be human?
Oh not because happiness exists,
Nor out of curiosity . . .
But because being here means so much;
because everything here,
vanishing so quickly, seems to need us,
and strangely keeps calling to us. . . . To have been
here once, completely, even if only once,
to have been at one with the earth——
this is beyond undoing.

RAINER MARIA RILKE

We live in precarious times. A traditional Tibetan exorcism chant, written many centuries ago, describes a dark age in terms that seem strangely fitting today:

An evil time, when relatives quarrel,
When there are family feuds and civil wars . . .
[Provoking the wrath of the Furies, who respond by]
Sending sickness on man and beast.
The sky is thick with purple clouds of sickness.
They destroy by causing the age of weaponry.
Suddenly, they strike men with fatal ulcerous sores . . .

Everywhere we look, forces of disintegration seem to have the upper hand, with organizations at every level—from schools and religious communities to cities and nations—seemingly unable to function sanely or to foster healthy human development. All across the planet we find a staggering array of symptoms of loss of soul, both in individuals and in the world at large. Our very humanness seems to be under assault and at risk. So many aspects of modern life—the destruction of the environment, the loss of neighborhood and community, the decline of education, the production of devitalized food, the meaningless work so many people perform, the rise of random violence, the blind allegiance to technological "progress" without consideration of its terrible costs, the fascination with glamor, hype, and image, the pervasive political lies and media distortions that masquerade as truth, the desecration of the sacred lands and traditions of native peoples, the descent into growing chaos and poverty among much of the world's population, the concentration of power in the hands of transnational corporations that have little interest in the common good, and on and on, wherever we turn our gaze—suggest that humanity has sold its soul in a Faustian exchange for worldly dominion, and that the payment is rapidly coming due.

And if we look within ourselves, we find turmoil and confusion: Our minds and hearts have either grown numb or are running wild. We have lost our bearings.

What is the significance of intimate relationship in a time like this? Can the love between intimate partners have a part to play in the regeneration of the planet, or the awakening of humanity from its collective trance? What can two lovers do to help this fractured world?

Learning to Live with a Broken Heart

Loving another deeply helps us appreciate the power and beauty of being human: the grace of the body, the clarity of awareness, the subtlety of feeling, and the richness of presence available to us. Yet when we turn from this inner vision—of the essential goodness at the core of our nature—to outer reality—the ragged state of the world and our fellow beings—it breaks our heart right on the spot.

Perhaps our first impulse is to turn away, close our eyes to the magnitude of suffering all around, and withdraw into our cocoon, turning to relationship as an island of refuge from a world gone mad. This is understandable. We feel overwhelmed.

But there is also another impulse, which we may have felt when we were young and our heart first registered the shock of human suffering: *We would like to save the world.* We would like to do something to make everything right, to clean up the environment, to overcome ignorance and injustice, or to help people tormented by poverty or despair. If we stay with this impulse for a moment, before dismissing it as hopelessly romantic or idealistic, we recognize it as the heart's pure response to the pain of this world.

Yet it soon becomes clear that we cannot readily save anyone, much less ourselves, from this pain. If we are to remain open to life and capable of engaging with our world rather than succumbing to depression or cynicism, we must learn how to live with a broken heart.

It is only through letting our heart break that we discover something unexpected: The heart cannot actually *break*, it can only break *open*. What breaks when we are touched by life's pain is the contraction around our heart that we have been carrying for so long. When we feel both our love for this world and the pain of this world—together, at the same time—the heart *breaks out* of this shell. Then the heart's true character is revealed—as an openness, an acute sensitivity where we feel the world inside us and are not separate from it. This is like removing a bandage and exposing our flesh to the air. There is no way to avoid this rawness, except by living in a state of contraction. To live with a broken-open heart is to experience life full strength.

Facing the condition of our world with an open heart is something like the situation of the man in the Zen story who is chased over the edge of a cliff by a tiger. As he holds on for dear life to some branches growing on the face of the cliff, he notices a mouse gnawing away at their roots. The man sizes up his predicament: hungry tiger above, yawning abyss below, and all support rapidly eroding away. Just as he is about to give himself up for lost, he notices some wild strawberries growing in the branches. Suddenly revived, he reaches out to taste the tiny berries, delighting in their outrageous sweetness.

Like the man in this story, we are tempted to give up when we find no simple remedy for the degenerative forces sweeping across our planet. Yet in moments when we can reach out and celebrate life's beauty, in spite of its pain or sorrow, we discover something sweet indeed—our own wild and beautiful heart.

According to sacred tradition, the heart is not something emotional or sentimental; Hinduism and Buddhism regard it as the pith essence, while Sufism understands it as a divine subtlety that reveals the deepest truths. It is a doorway leading into the core of our being—the living presence of spirit and soul. When our heart breaks *open*, breaks *through* to this deeper core, we waken from paralysis into a greater depth of soul, and along with that, a deeper love for this world.

For if our heart gives rise to universal compassion, it is in our soul that we love particulars—*this* face, *this* grove of trees, *this* neighborhood, *this* world. And it is our soul that suffers when, for instance, we see a beautiful, wild piece of the earth fall prey to yet another condo development or shopping mall. Our heart might feel compassion for this injury, our spirit might recognize it as part of the larger life and death of the cosmos, but in our soul, which so loves the particulars, we grieve or rage for this assault on earth's beauty. It is important to let ourselves feel this kind of passionate response. Otherwise, our soul too grows numb, just like the paved-over patch of earth.

To avoid going numb when encountering the pain of the world, we need access to the warrior within, the one who can ask: "What deeper resource is this adversity calling on me to bring forth?" In learning to make use of suffering to cultivate our capacities for strength, vision, love, faith, or humor, we forge the vessel of soul and begin to free ourselves from resentment or depression about the state of the world. And we may find that the earth in her plight is calling us to waken like this, and that as we do so, she awakens as well, through us. In this way, the broken-hearted warrior is able to keep on loving, in spite of everything.

When the heart breaks open, it marks the beginning of a real love affair with this world. It is a broken-hearted love affair, rather than the conventional kind based on hope and expectation. Only in this fearless love that can respond to life's pain as well as its beauty can we be of real help to ourselves or anyone else in this difficult age. The broken-hearted warrior is an essential archetype for our time.

Taking Up the Path

What better place to set out on such a path than in relation to the one I love most, whose heart I have broken open, and who in turn has broken mine open on so many occasions? Here with her I have seen all my angels and demons rise up before me. I have tried to find salvation and failed, and have discovered hidden treasure where I least expected it. I have run in terror and have been the terrorist. I have cursed my partner and fallen down beside her in gratitude. I have been stunned by the truth of her words and the deceit in my own heart. I have imagined her to be my enemy and known her to be my greatest friend. We have danced and played and cried together long into the night. And the deeper our love grows, the more mindful I am of death's silent, relentless approach.

Letting the heart break open not only allows me to engage more fully with my partner and with the world, it also keeps bringing me back to home-ground, reminding me that I can only be as *there* with another as I am *here* with myself. No matter how much I might like to make something outside me responsible for how I feel, the heart speaks a different truth. It reminds me that the joys and sorrows of relationship are only happening here, where I feel utterly raw and open. As long as I see love as dependent on something "out there," I will experience it as a passing *state* at best—a good feeling that comes and goes—but never as a stable *station*—an intrinsic quality of my being.

If "a fool sees self as Other," as Zen master Dogen once said, then we must all be fools. In turning away from our basic openness, we throw away our own jewellike essence, and then express that alienation in everything we do. This is what is impoverishing our collective soul. This is the plague that is ravaging humanity.

We cannot heal our alienation from ourselves through some strategy or technique. Approaching it in that way only perpetuates inner division—between me as problem solver and myself as a problem to be solved—which *is* the problem in the first place. Self-hatred can only be *dissolved* by taking it to heart, letting its pain come to full consciousness in body and soul. Then this ignites a holy desire—to open our heart to ourselves at last.

When Dogen goes on to say that "a wise man sees Other as self," he indicates the salvation our world most needs. We need to reclaim and make friends with whatever we have made Other inside. Then we will naturally start to love and care for what we have made Other *outside* as well—our beautiful, broken world.

As two lovers break open their hearts and cultivate a greater depth of soul through their connection, they will also feel the soullessness of the modern world more keenly. Yet here is where they really have something to give: by working to bring heart and soul back into this world. They might start by making their home a sacred environment, nurturing the deeper humanness in their children, or cultivating a community of caring friends. Then they might extend further, by bringing greater open-heartedness and humanness into their everyday dealings with people, helping others wake up from the forces of numbing and soullessness taking over the world, by caring for the place on earth they inhabit, by turning away from soul-depleting influences like television and devoting more time to real conversation, meditation, spiritual practice, or creativity, or by dedicating their lives to serving the forces of awakening and renewal in our society at large. These are but a few of the countless ways that lovers could start to expand their vision and their love. If they can let their relationship serve as a vessel that nurtures soul, and can share with others what they discover as they heal their own inner divisions, this could be one of the greatest gifts they offer this acrimonious world.

In this way intimate relationship becomes a microcosm where we can learn to break open our heart for the sake of all beings. In learning to soften with our pain, to open to our fear, to celebrate the beauty of life despite all its sorrows, we step out of the prison of our conditioning. We set out on a path that is continually surprising—learning to be ourselves, yet also more than ourselves. As Zen master Shunryu Suzuki points out, "When you are yourself, just yourself, through and through, you are the universe. You are not this conditioned person anymore." Then, though we may dedicate ourselves to helping this world, our well-being will not depend on the outcome. For we are becoming one with that force in the universe that is forever creating itself anew.

ACKNOWLEDGMENTS

M y work with relationships is the outgrowth of a lifelong concern with the interface between the psychological and the spiritual. As such, it represents the convergence of many different streams of influence. I would like to acknowledge here some of those, living and dead, who have influenced me and helped shape my thinking, though in truth there are too many to name them all.

I am indebted to the existential philosophers for first articulating loss of being as the central problem of our time, and recovery of being as our central challenge. In my early twenties their work spoke to me like none other, and first helped me make sense of my life. The existential psychotherapists pointed the way for me as a therapist, by defining the healing relationship as a disclosure of being that can help people free themselves from the past and find their true individuality and sense of purpose. I am especially grateful to Eugene Gendlin, who first opened up the realm of inner experience for me, and brought home the existentialist concerns in an immediate, personal way.

On the spiritual side, I am forever indebted to the great teachers of the Kagyu and Nyingma lineages of Tibet, who have so generously shared a wisdom that was once reserved for only a select few, and particularly Chögyam Trungpa and Tsoknyi Rinpoche for revealing to me the vast space of being and how it can be entered directly on the spot. More recently, I have also been influenced by the direct approach of Ramana Maharshi, as well as by the work of Hameed Ali, which I find convergent with my own in many ways.

I particularly want to acknowledge my wife, Jennifer, for her generous love and encouragement, which helped me continue to persevere and stay on track with this book at every stage along the way. Through her presence in my life as a partner and co-teacher, she also contributed important ideas and helped me clarify my thinking during the years of bringing this work to fruition. And while we chose not to single out her input from my own, she was also an important participant in many of the dialogues in this book. She was my most incisive and hardest-working editor as well, going over the manuscript many times in different drafts.

I would also like to thank Barry Spacks for his helpful editing of the whole manuscript, as well as Stephan Bodian, Paul Shippee, and Barbara Green, who provided useful feedback on various chapters.

NOTES

Introduction

P. xii, *The time is ripe for couples' consciousness-raising:* We are the first people in history who can actually consider such a possibility. Complete freedom to choose a life partner has only been widely available for less than a hundred years in the West—just a few generations. People could not even discuss sex frankly and openly before the 1930s (the first Western sex manual appeared in 1929). And it was not until the fifties and sixties, when pop psychology books first appeared, that large numbers of people finally had access to language and information that enabled them to think and talk about the interpersonal dynamics of relationships.

Until recent times, there was never a great need to develop greater consciousness in the area of intimate relationship because family and society held the vision of marriage, strictly defining and enforcing its rules and roles. As long as families controlled courtship and marriage, couple consciousness never had to evolve. In many extended families and tribes, couples were like children still at home: They lived by the rules and did what they were told.

As the family's influence began to wane in the industrial era, children's desire for greater freedom gave rise to a revolutionary new form of mate selection: dating. With the advent of dating in the 1920s, couple consciousness entered a new stage of development, which we could liken to adolescence. Suddenly couples had a new task—to discover how to establish lasting ties based on personal feelings and passions. Starting in the 1920s, the starstruck lovers of movies and soap operas epitomized this adolescent stage, which is often marked by rebellion against tradition and by dreams of perfect love. It reached a climax in the 1960s, which exploded with every conceivable kind of sexual experiment. Like most adolescent escapades, this was a period of trial and error that set the stage for further developments.

At the verge of a new millennium, couple consciousness is finally ready to move into adulthood. If safety and security mark the child stage of relationship, and freedom, rebellion, and excitement mark the adolescent phase, the birth of the adult stage requires couples to develop a deeper consciousness of who they are and what they are doing together.

P. xv, *spiritual bypassing:* For more on this concept, see the article where I first coined this term, "Principles of Inner Work: Psychological and Spiritual," *Journal of Transpersonal Psychology,* 16 (1), 1984.

Chapter One

P. 4, *Chögyam Trungpa had a revealing term:* See C. Trungpa, *Shambhala: the Sacred Path of the Warrior* (Boston: Shambhala, 1984).

P. 5, *William Butler Yeats . . . had a vivid experience:* From W. B. Yeats, "Vacillation" in *Collected Poems of W.B. Yeats* (London: Macmillan, 1955).

Chapter Two

P. 9, *Hermann Hesse wrote:* H. Hesse, "Iris," in H. Hesse, *Strange News from Another Star,* translated by D. Lindley (New York: Farrar, Straus, & Giroux, 1972). All the quotations from this story are from this edition.

P. 10, *Anselm is unwittingly connecting with the depth of his soul:* I am not suggesting that young children have full access to their deeper spiritual nature, which is then lost during the course of development. Soul, our individual way of expressing our essential nature (as described more fully in chapter 4) is not fully present in childhood, but rather develops over a lifetime. Nonetheless, children may have glimpses of this deeper nature, even though they may not fully recognize or understand its significance.

P. 10, *the Indian sage Aurobindo:* Quoted in Satprem, *Sri Aurobindo: The Adventure of Consciousness* (Pondicherry, India: Sri Aurobindo Ashram Trust, 1968), p. 91.

P. 11, *We have not yet developed the self-reflective awareness:* Reflective awareness—the ability to step back and fully consider our experience—does not fully ripen until the early teen-age years, during a stage of development that child psychologist Jean Piaget called "formal operations." Lacking this capacity, young children cannot clearly understand themselves or their experience. Nor can they fully appreciate the valuable, lovable qualities of their nature if their parents or other adults do not reflect these back to them.

To help children develop their larger potential, the adult world would ideally provide two kinds of recognition—of a child's individual qualities and universal nature as well. My wife's father, for example, gave her a stuffed lion when she was three and told her that she was like this lion: beautiful, strong, and radiant. She still remembers this as a special moment in her childhood, for it served as a blessing in which her father let her know that he saw and encouraged her particular soul-qualities.

In addition, children also need to have their larger, universal nature reflected back to them. In traditional societies, this was the province of religion. In the brahminical caste of India, for example, a child of five traditionally began studies with a family guru, or spiritual guide. In this way, children were directly introduced to and taught about their divine nature.

In the Tibetan Buddhist tradition, young children believed to be reincarnated enlightened beings—they are called *tulkus*—were taken to a monastery at an early age for a complete spiritual education. One of the most important teachings that Tibetan teachers provide is called the "pointing-out instruction," in which the master reveals and helps the student recognize the true nature and power of his or her own being. Judging from those teachers I have met who received this kind of instruction in their youth, I have to conclude that it has profound results—for these are the most powerful spiritual beings I have ever come across. I have also heard Tibetan teachers claim that when such a tulku is not recognized and given this kind of education, he may live a lost, confused life.

P. 14, *This confining room is our ego or conditioned personality:* I am not using the term *ego* in the strict clinical sense—as the overall capacity for functioning, but more loosely, to mean a frozen self-concept based on past conditioning. (In the strict psychoanalytic sense, the self-concept is only one of the ego's functions—its self-representational capacity.) For the purposes of simplicity, clarity, and readability, I am not trying to present a precise or comprehensive picture of ego development here, but only a bare-bones view of how the self-concept typically forms and develops.

When I use the term *personality*, I mean *conditioned personality*, a view of ourselves based on past conditioning. But through the process of soulwork described in chapter four, there could also develop a "soul-infused" personality—a personal way of living that is open to, and draws on, one's larger, divine nature.

P. 14,   *waking dream or trance that we come to live within:* Pinpointing the psychological genesis of our identity-trances provides a more concrete understanding of the teaching found in all the great spiritual traditions: that most of humanity lives in a state of sleep.

P. 14,   *Emily Dickinson describes:* There are two slightly different versions of this poem in existence. This version is from M. D. Bianchi and A. L. Hampson (eds.), *Poems by Emily Dickinson* (Boston: Little, Brown & Co., 1937).

P. 17,   *we stand on a razor's edge:* For a fuller discussion of the razor's edge and its central importance in relationships, see *Journey of the Heart*, chapter 5.

P. 20,   *As Hesse puts it:* H. Hesse, *Reflections*, translated by R. Manheim (New York: Farrar, Straus, & Giroux, 1974), p. 168.

Chapter Three

P. 33,   *this more painful, threatening unconscious identity:* "Unconscious" here means that the identity operates in the background of awareness and is not usually noticed. Sometimes these identities can be readily uncovered and brought into awareness with just a little attention and effort (in which case we might more properly call them "subconscious"). In other cases, they remain more deeply buried, and come to light only after prolonged or intensive self-inquiry.

P. 36,   *As our mind fixates on these impressions:* The metaphor of the wax is only meant to suggest that our nature is highly impressionable, *not* that our mind is a *tabula rasa*, a blank slate totally conditioned by external forces. Children are also born with their own innate tendencies, and their minds play an active role in selecting, interpreting, and responding to the information they take in.

    Although most of us receive faulty mirroring from our parents, we each respond to that in our own way and do something different with it. In the same situation one child might become compliant and strive to please, another might fight and rebel, and another might withdraw or become depressed. Such different reactions are in part the result of innate tendencies in the child's own makeup.

    In the West these innate tendencies are explained in terms of heredity and in the East as karma—and they probably influence how our parents respond to us as well. Thus childhood conditioning arises out of a mutual interaction between parent and child. How we fixate on and internalize what happens between self and Other in childhood, and what we do with that in later life, is *our* karma. It is also what we will have to work out in our intimate relationships.

P. 36, *our parents reflect back to us certain pictures of who we are in their eyes:* As the British psychoanalyst and pediatrician Winnicott once wrote, "In individual development, the precursor of the mirror is the mother's face." (Quoted in H. M. Southwood, "The Origin of Self-Awareness and Ego Behavior," *International Journal of Psychoanalysis,* 54 [1973], p. 237.)

P. 36, *Lacking our own self-reflective awareness:* The influence of parents on children is especially pronounced in a culture like ours, where children do not grow up in a larger extended family or tribe, continually exposed to a wide range of different interactions with adults. Also, in traditional cultures, if parents could not recognize the soul qualities of a child, at least the culture itself provided ways to nurture soul— through myth, ritual, storytelling, spiritual teachings, or initiation practices that would help young people see and understand the meaningfulness of their life in relation to the larger cosmos. Today, however, we live in what Christopher Lasch termed a "culture of narcissism"—which promotes and glorifies images of the false self.

P. 36, *To form an identity means:* Spiritual teacher A. H. Almaas provides a clear description of this process of identification:

"To identify with anything, any state, means simply that . . . your mind holds on to an expression, or a feeling, or a state, and uses it to define you. The mind then contracts around the state in the activity of holding on to it. This very contraction of the mind creates what we call 'identity.' So identifying with something is taking a concept and saying 'That's me' or 'That defines me.'" (*Diamond Heart,* vol. 3, *Being and the Meaning of Life* [Berkeley: Almaas Publications, 1990], pp. 170–1.)

Because of these identifications, by the time consciousness matures in the teenage years, children are already saddled with the burden of seeing themselves in a number of limited, distorted ways. In adulthood, it takes conscious work to awaken from these old identifications. Unfortunately, most adults never manage to do so.

P. 37, *we may develop a view of ourselves:* The technical term for this view of ourselves is "self-representation."

Chapter Four

P. 50, *French writer Suzanne Lilar:* S. Lilar, *Aspects of Love in Western Society,* translated by Jonathan Griffin (London: Thames and Hudson, 1965). The selection in which this quotation appears was reprinted in J. Welwood (ed.), *Challenge of the Heart* (Boston: Shambhala, 1985), p. 232.

P. 50, *Soul, as I am using this term:* I introduce the term *soul* here gingerly because it has been used in so many different ways in so many different traditions, often without being clearly defined, that it has become a fuzzy, ambiguous term. Or else it remains limited by the particular associations of a given tradition. It is especially problematic when used as a pat explanation for the mysteries of human experience, or when it is assumed to be some immortal, fully formed substance within the body.

As defined here, soul is not something "in" the body. Rather, it is a way of referring to what animates the body—our individual, embodied beingness, the living process that we are, with roots in the universal. It is, in Sri Aurobindo's words, "a spark of the divine." Thus I am defining soul more broadly than many Jungians, who see it more narrowly as the activity or contents of imagination.

For those in the Buddhist tradition who might be uncomfortable with the word *soul,* I would suggest that this term is akin to what that tradition calls the Rupakaya— the "form body," the particular character and qualities that an individual manifests. This is distinguished from the Dharmakaya, the "Dharma body," which is universal, the same in everyone. While the Dharmakaya remains impersonal and unchanging, the Rupakaya evolves and ripens in time, through the development of our essential human qualities and virtues. This ripening is what I am calling soulwork here—the development of the larger qualities of our humanness (described in the Buddhist tradition as the "accumulation of merit"). This is distinct from the realization of Dharmakaya, which happens through directly seeing into our true nature (the "accumulation of wisdom"). Thus the difference between Rupakaya and Dharmakaya is roughly analogous to the distinction between soul and spirit in the Western esoteric tradition.

From a slightly different perspective, soul is analogous to the Sambhogakaya, the "aliveness-body," which is intermediate between the "form-body" of the Nirmanakaya and the formless "essence-body" of the Dharmakaya.

P. 51, *In the words of the Sufi poet Rumi:* Rumi, "Opening," in *One-Handed Basket Weaving,* translated by C. Barks (Athens, Ga.: Maypop, 1991).

P. 52, *As the Indian poet Tagore:* R. Tagore, "The Circle," in *Some Songs and Poems from Rabindranath Tagore,* translated by P. Bowes (London: East West Publications, 1984).

P. 53, *soul evolves and deepens through cultivating and embodying the seed potentials:* These capacities are innate, rather than learned. Love, for example, just arises; no one has to teach us how to feel it. We can learn to extend our love more broadly, or to remove the barriers in its way, but love itself emerges as an intrinsic quality of our being. The same is true for our other human capacities, such as courage, strength, patience, humor, dedication, equanimity. Nonetheless, many of these capacities often remain unrealized because our conditioned personality blocks our access to them. In that case, they remain dormant seeds that never receive the water or sunlight necessary to bear fruit.

P. 53, *Rilke once described the soulwork:* R. M. Rilke, *Letters to a Young Poet*, translated by M. D. Herter Norton (New York: Norton, 1954). Reprinted in J. Welwood, *Challenge of the Heart*, p. 258.

P. 60, *Chögyam Trungpa defines warrior:* C. Trungpa, *Shambhala: The Sacred Path of the Warrior*, p. 28.

P. 61, *In Trungpa's words:* C. Trungpa, ibid, pp. 49–50.

Chapter Five

P. 64, *Since it is painful to acknowledge this "bad self":* I am using the term *bad self* to mean a particular kind of unconscious identity, rather than in the strict way it is defined in object relations theory, as a form of the more primitive defense of splitting.

P. 66, *Yet even if we do win this approval:* Since unconditional goodness is not something that could ever be earned or possessed, trying to prove our value only separates us further from it.

P. 70, *Loving-kindness is a term often used in the Buddhist tradition:* The term is *maitri* in Sanskrit, *metta* in Pali.

P. 72, *this usually indicates that some story:* For a further discussion of what I mean by the term *story*, and the difference between stories and felt experience, see *Journey of the Heart*, chapter 2.

P. 74, *Chögyam Trungpa describes drala:* C. Trungpa, *Shambhala: The Sacred Path of the Warrior*, p. 107.

Chapter Six

P. 104, *I call this fourfold truth:* Fourfold truth is a more structured form of truth-telling and self-revelation, which are discussed more fully in chapter 9.

Chapter Seven

P. 114, *the Hasidic sage:* M. Buber, *Tales of the Hasidim* (New York: Schocken, 1947), p. 104. The "between-stage" is also considered important in the Tibetan Buddhist tradition, where it is known as the *bardo* state. Usually we don't notice these transitional moments, these unstructured gaps between two more definable states of consciousness, such as between two thoughts, or in the passage between work and rest. In meditation practice, these gaps provide a glimpse of freedom from the driving current of thoughts that usually sweeps us along. The Tibetan tradition also teaches that we enter a bardo at the time of dying, and that if we do not know how to let go of old fixations at that time, our consciousness will be thrown into states of terror and confusion that will affect what happens to us after death. Therefore it is important to notice the bardos in our life and learn to navigate through them.

P. 116, *what psychologist Eugene Gendlin calls a felt sense:* For a further discussion of how to work with a felt sense, see Eugene Gendlin, *Focusing* (New York: Bantam, 1981). See also my articles: "The Unfolding of Experience," *Journal of Humanistic Psychology*, 22 (1), 1982, and "Reflections on Focusing, Psychotherapy, and Meditation," in J. Welwood (ed.), *Awakening the Heart* (Boston: Shambhala, 1983).

Those who know the Focusing method will recognize elements of it in my description of the work with Anna. Yet Focusing is a more goal-oriented, step-by-step technique than the more open-ended way I generally work with clients. For a further discussion of my method, see "The Healing Power of Unconditional Presence," in J. Welwood (ed.), *Ordinary Magic: Everyday Life as Spiritual Path* (Boston: Shambhala, 1992).

Chapter Eight

P. 124, *negative negativity:* C. Trungpa, *The Myth of Freedom* (Boston: Shambhala, 1976), p. 73.

Chapter Nine

P. 131, *the Argument that keeps recurring:* Some couples who cannot resolve their Argument wind up avoiding conflict altogether, creating a superficial harmony that stifles the vital energy between them.

P. 132, *According to psychologist James Hillman:* J. Hillman and M. Ventura, *We've Had a Hundred Years of Psychotherapy and the World's Getting Worse* (San Francisco: HarperCollins, 1992), p. 99.

Chapter Ten

P. 161, *In the ancient Chinese view of the genders:* Of course there are many exceptions to this generalization. I am by no means suggesting that women should live up to some yin ideal, men to some yang ideal. The various ways in which men and women combine and embody these two energies invariably lead to a wide range of different individual expressions. In fact, there are ways in which men are more yin than women, and women more yang than men, as discussed further in chapter 11. The polytheistic religions portray this variety in pantheons that contain not only yang gods (Ares) and yin goddesses (Aphrodite), but also goddesses who are more yang (Athena, Artemis) and gods who are more yin (Adonis, Dionysus).

In addition to their different blends of yin and yang, the distinct psychologies of men and women are also shaped by different biological, cultural, and historical forces. Because of the wide range of differences in individual temperament and conditioning, be it understood that when I refer to the various characteristic ways of men and women in this book, I mean most, but by no means all, men or women in our culture.

Finally, it should be emphasized that the qualities attributed to masculine and feminine are not hard-and-fast, written-in-stone differences. Not every culture divides them in the way that Western and Chinese cultures do.

For a fuller discussion of this whole issue, see *Journey of the Heart*, chapter 12.

P. 162, *the outer form of marriage:* In *Journey of the Heart* I distinguished three dimensions of marriage—outer, inner, and secret. Here, for the sake of simplicity, I am using the term *inner marriage* to refer to both the inner and the secret dimensions that I discussed there. See chapter 15 of that book for a fuller discussion of the deeper meaning and purpose of marriage.

P. 164, *as D. H. Lawrence points out:* D. H. Lawrence, "Blessed Are the Powerful," in W. Roberts and H. Moore (eds.), *Phoenix II: Uncollected, Unpublished, and Other Prose Works* (New York: Viking, 1970).

P. 167, *the feminine has been debased:* Aside from all the well-publicized problems resulting from the belittling of the feminine, another symptom is a crisis of faith: We have difficulty trusting the goodness of life or the human heart. Post-modern cynicism and irony have become the fashionable defenses of the day.

P. 170, *Wisdom is regarded as feminine:* "Does not wisdom call, does not understanding raise her voice? On the heights beside the way, in the paths she takes her stand; beside the gates in front of the town, at the entrance of the portals she cries aloud: 'To you, O men, I call, and my cry is to the sons of men . . . By me kings reign and nobles govern the earth'" (*Proverbs*, 8:1–17). Here we see that wisdom is the feminine ground that allows the masculine to function properly ("by me kings reign . . . "). And in the following lines from *The Book of Wisdom*, we see Solomon relating to Sophia as his lover: "Wisdom I loved; I sought her out when I was young and longed to win her for my bride, and I fell in love with her beauty" (*Wisdom*, 8: 2).

Chapter Eleven

P. 182, *psychologist Lillian Rubin:* L. Rubin, *Intimate Strangers* (New York: HarperCollins, 1983). The selection in which this quotation appears was reprinted in J. Welwood (ed.), *Challenge of the Heart*, pp. 126–7.

P. 185, *In Rilke's words:* R. M. Rilke, *Letters to a Young Poet*, translated by M. D. Herter Norton (New York: Norton, 1954). The selection in which this quotation appears was reprinted in J. Welwood (ed.), *Challenge of the Heart*, p. 262.

P. 188, *the wrathful dakini:* For a further discussion of the dakini, see *Journey of the Heart*, chapter 12. For a discussion of beginner's mind, see the introduction and chapter 10 of that book.

P. 189, *In their brief marriage, C. S. Lewis:* C. S. Lewis, *A Grief Observed* (New York: Seabury Press, 1961), p. 8.

P. 189, *Women are the supreme fire of transformation:* From an Indian Tantric text cited in M. Shaw, *Passionate Enlightenment: Women in Tantric Buddhism* (Princeton, N.J.: Princeton University Press, 1994).

P. 193, *Delilah seems to represent:* For a further discussion of this "black witch" element in women, see *Journey of the Heart*, chapter 13.

P. 193, *Philosopher Julius Evola:* J. Evola, *The Metaphysics of Sex* (New York: Inner Traditions, 1983), p. 167.

P. 194, *The first and foremost knight:* H. Pyle, *The Story of King Arthur and His Knights* (New York: Scribner's, 1903), p. 144.

Dialogue Eleven A

P. 204, *when he honors her like this:* There have been important historical moments when a man's devotion to a woman suddenly took on great importance and value—during the rise of Tantric Buddhism in Asia and courtly love in Southern France—ushering in powerful periods of artistic creativity and spiritual innovation. In these two traditions, a lover's relation to his beloved was marked by honor and praise, service and adoration, instead of the dominance and disregard that usually prevailed. Exalting the feminine was seen as a spiritual practice that could open a man's heart, refine his character, and unlock a wealth of creative wisdom and energy. Of course, this can't just be a one-way street today, as it was for the courtly lovers. Men and women could both learn to celebrate each other's gifts and serve one another in different ways.

Chapter Twelve

P. 221, *D. H. Lawrence suggests:* D. H. Lawrence, *John Thomas and Lady Jane* (New York: Viking, 1972), pp. 107–8.

P. 221, *the Japanese philosopher Nishitani:* K. Nishitani, *Religion and Nothingness*, translated by J. Van Bragt (Los Angeles: University of California Press, 1982.

P. 223, *This is the exalted melancholy of our fate:* M. Buber, *I and Thou*, translated by R. G. Smith (New York, Scribner's, 1958).

Chapter Thirteen

P. 229, *Antonio Machado describes this:* A. Machado, "Last Night," translated by R. Bly, in *Times Alone: Selected Poems of Antonio Machado* (Middletown, Conn.: Wesleyan University Press, 1983).

P. 230, *According to Chögyam Trungpa, renunciation:* C. Trungpa, *Shambhala: The Sacred Path of the Warrior*, pp. 66, 69, 84.

Chapter Fourteen

P. 237, *The broken-hearted warrior:* The idea of the warrior with a broken heart comes from C. Trungpa, *Shambhala*, p. 69.

FURTHER READINGS

For further reading, related to major themes discussed in this book, I particularly recommend the following:

Almaas, A. H. *Essence*. York Beach, Me.: Weiser, 1986.
An illuminating study of the loss of being in childhood and its recovery through inner work.

Chödron, P. *Start Where You Are*. Boston: Shambhala, 1994.
A beautiful book on cultivating loving-kindness.

Gendlin, E. *Focusing*. New York: Bantam, 1981.
A clear and simple introduction to the Focusing method, an extremely helpful way of bringing awareness to unclear or difficult feelings, staying present with them, and inquiring into them to uncover new directions.

Trungpa, C. *Shambhala: The Sacred Path of the Warrior*. Boston: Shambhala, 1984.
A powerful, inspiring, clear presentation of the path of the warrior, grounded in meditation practice.

Welwood, J. (ed.). *Awakening the Heart: East/West Approaches to Psychotherapy and the Healing Relationship*. Boston: Shambhala, 1983.
An East/West framework for working with different states of mind and emotion—our own and those of others.

Welwood, J. (ed.). *Challenge of the Heart: Love, Sex, and Intimacy in Changing Times*. Boston: Shambhala, 1985.

A companion collection of writings on relationship, some of the most useful I came across while working on *Journey of the Heart*.

Welwood, J. *Journey of the Heart: The Path of Conscious Love.* New York: HarperCollins, 1990.

A broad overview and exploration of relationship as a path of personal and spiritual development, this book also addresses certain areas more fully than *Love and Awakening* does, including: passion, surrender, commitment, wildness, beginner's mind, aloneness, marriage, sex, male/female issues, sacredness, the razor's edge, breaking open the heart, the nature of path, and the relevance of meditation to relationship.

Welwood, J. (ed.). *Ordinary Magic: Everyday Life as Spiritual Path.* Boston: Shambhala, 1992.

A lively collection of writings on discovering the sacred dimension in many different aspects of daily life.

Wile, D. *After the Honeymoon: How Conflict Can Improve Your Relationship.* New York: Wiley, 1988.

The most useful practical book on couple communication I have found.

We teach occasional workshops on intimate relationship as a sacred path, based on the principles and practices presented in this book. These workshops, which include meditation practice and other experiential methods, are offered primarily in the San Francisco Bay Area, but sometimes in other locations as well.

Our work with relationship is also part of a larger concern with psychological work in the service of spiritual development. We plan to present this larger body of teaching through a formal training program—in Presence-Centered Counseling and Psychotherapy™—for health professionals and interested laypeople.

If you would like to be on our mailing list, please contact:

Journey of the Heart Seminars
P.O. Box 2173
Mill Valley, CA 94942
415-381-6077